HISTORY, PEOPLE AND PLACES IN
PROVENCE

Auguste Renoir's home, studio and garden at Cagnes-sur-Mer

HISTORY, PEOPLE AND PLACES IN
PROVENCE

A. N. BRANGHAM

SPURBOOKS LIMITED

PUBLISHED BY SPURBOOKS LTD 6 PARADE COURT BOURNE END BUCKINGHAMSHIRE

© A.N. BRANGHAM 1976

All Rights Reserved: No part of this publication may be reproduced, stored in a retrieval system, or transmitted in any form or by any means, electronic, photocopying, recording or otherwise, without the permission of the publisher.

ISBN 0 904978 15 X

Designed and produced by Mechanick Exercises, London

Typesetting by Inforum, Portsmouth
Printed in Great Britain by Chapel River Press, Andover

CONTENTS

	Illustrations	6
	Acknowledgements	9
1	Introduction to the country's character	11
2	Historical perspectives	24
3	Approach from the north: Rhône Valley and Tricastin	40
4	Bastion of the Alps: around Mont Ventoux	53
5	Withdrawn hills: the Lubéron range	64
6	The Virgilian Alpilles	73
7	Arles and the Camargue	85
8	Inspiration for art: Montagne Sainte-Victoire	99
9	From Sisteron to the sea	108
10	East of the Durance	120
11	The Riviera	127
12	In and around Marseille	136
13	Alpine valleys and Azur coast	144
	Bibliography	156
	Index	159

ILLUSTRATIONS

Auguste Renoir's home, studio and garden at Cagnes-sur-Mer	*frontispiece*
Olives and sunsmitten hills near St. Rémy-de-Provence	12
Subtropical vegetation at Monaco	14
Hostile environment: sun, drought, salt in the Camargue	16
A characteristic village: Puyméras in Vaucluse	19
Brantes dwarfed by the north flank of Mont Ventoux	21
The human scale: Chapelle St. Sixte, Eygalières	22
Transhumance on foot, a vanishing tradition	25
Black bulls of the Camargue	28
An afternoon's harmless sport for boys and bulls	29
Ile St. Honorat, from the 4th century an influential religious centre	30
Effigies of the two Marys at Les Saintes-Maries-de-la-Mer	31
Eze, medieval bastion against sea-bôrne invaders	32
Tarascon castle guarding the Rhone	34
Bravade at St. Tropez, the annual mid-June celebrations	36
Grasse, capital of the perfume industry	38
Harvesting grapes near the Var coast	41
Orange, a performance in the floodlit Roman theatre	46
Orange, the splendidly preserved Roman arch	48
Avignon, Palace of the Popes and the Rhône	50
Vaison-la-Romaine and the excavations	54
Fontaine de Vaucluse and the resurgent river Sorgue	57
A parched country, yet every village has its fountain: Vence	58
Dentelles de Montmirail and Mont Ventoux beyond	61
Notre Dame d'Aubune near Beaumes-de-Venise (Vaucluse)	62
The river Durance, the artery of Provence	66
Sénanque (Vaucluse), one of three Cistercian abbeys	68

Gordes (Vaucluse), slowly restored by artists	71
Roman arch outside St. Rémy-de-Provence	74
Roman mausoleum outside St. Rémy-de-Provence	75
The site of *Glanum* backed by the Alpilles	76
Vincent Van Gogh's asylum: cloister of Prieuré de St. Paul de Mausole	79
Ruined Les Baux clings to the weathered Alpilles	82
Arles, Museum of Christian Art: Carvings on a 4th century sarcophagus	87
Les Alyscamps at Arles	89
The west porch of St. Trophime at Arles	90
Camargue *gardians* on white horses, perhaps first brought by Saracens	93
Thatched *gardian* huts in the Camargue	94
Fortress church of Les Saintes Maries-de-la-Mer	95
Curtain walls of Aigues-Mortes	96
Southern face of Montagne Sainte-Victoire	100
Aix-en-Provence, birthplace of Cézanne: Fontaine des Quatre Dauphins	104
Cloister of cathedral of St. Sauveur, Aix-en-Provence	106
Citadel of Sisteron, gateway into Provence	109
Typical wrought-iron cupola: Notre Dame, Manosque	112
Le Thoronet abbey, a restoration faithful to the original	115
Like penitents in procession, Rochers des Mées near the Durance	121
Remains of Roman temple to Apollo, Riez	122
Picturesquely sited Moustiers-Sainte-Marie	123
St. Tropez and its gulf	128
The boat for Corsica leaves Nice harbour	130
Calanque de Sormiou, a drowned valley near Marseille	131
Monaco, the modern skyline and Larvotto beach	133
Cannes and the Estérel range	134
Fisherman mending his net, Vallon des Auffes, Marseille	137
The Count of Monte Cristo's Château d'If	138
Marseille from the Palais Longchamp steps	139
Santons, painted clay figurines essential to a Provençal Christmas	141
I.B.M. research centre at La Gaude near Vence	145
Monaco: Oceanographic Museum directed by Jacques Cousteau	146
Henri Matisse's Chapelle du Rosaire at Vence	147

Potter at Vallauris; an industry revitalised by Pablo Picasso	149
Fondation Maeght, St. Paul; Giacometti figures in the courtyard	150
Partially restored Roman Trophy of the Alps, La Turbie	152
Bronze Age carvings on rocks of Val des Merveilles, Mont Bégo	153
Saorge suspended above the Roya river	154
Menton in the 'Bay of Peace' and the autoroute	155

ACKNOWLEDGEMENTS

The illustrations for this book have been supplied by the courtesy of the French Government Tourist Office in London. Behind this formal acknowledgement lies my appreciation of the unfailing help that has been given me by former colleagues and friends there, not least by Mrs. Pauline Hallam, Director of Public Relations.

1·INTRODUCTION TO THE COUNTRY'S CHARACTER

Let me first try and place Provence in its man-made context. It is an ancient province, part of a huge administrative region created by the Romans two thousand years ago. Its boundaries, expanding and contracting through a tumultuous history, were only finally fixed in 1947 when Tende and La Brigue voted to rejoin France from Italy. Today, it lies between the river Rhône and the Italian frontier, made up of the five *départements* (roughly approximating to our counties) of Bouches-du-Rhône, Var and Alpes-Maritimes; plus the inland *départements* of Vaucluse and Alpes de Haute-Provence (the latter, until a few years ago, more appropriately and modestly called Basses-Alpes). Together, these administrative units fill south-eastern France, south of a latitude drawn eastwards from around Pont St. Esprit on the Rhône. For centuries this town has been the traditional point of entry from the north into Provence when most travellers came by river in boats which had to sweep under one of the twenty-five arches of the medieval bridge.

This political definition sounds simple enough, yet there is plenty of disagreement over it. Some people, on aesthetic or historical grounds, deny Provençal legitimacy to the 'Italianate' Alpes-Maritimes (finally incorporated into France in 1860) with its 'degenerate' Côte d'Azur whose only genius, they say sourly, is its mediocrity. Others go further. They do not acknowledge any of the coast between Menton and Marseille as belonging to Provence which to them is a pure, Virgilian, inland landscape. Though if we accepted only what seems to be 'purely Virgilian' Provence would be minuscle indeed and shorn of its great variety. Then again, should the Gard, across the Rhône, be included? Its Roman monuments in Nîmes and the Pont du Gard are always thought of in the context of Provençal history. Yet Gard is in Languedoc, traditional rival to Provence; the

Olives and sunsmitten hills near St. Rémy-de-Provence

castles of Tarascon and Beaucaire still glare at one another across the river. I accept the Rhône as a frontier; there is a subtle difference between the two provinces, and so this book does not discuss Languedocian Gard. Other experts — and they include the French tourist authorities — incorporate Hautes-Alpes for reasons that escape me. How can Gap and Briançon be anything but part of the alpine complex? Conversely, who can deny that southern Drôme, northern neighbour to Vaucluse, feels Mediterranean in so many ways that it is mere pedantry to exclude it?

You see how passionate views about the place arise at the outset. People feel possessive about Provence, as though they alone upheld the truth. I am like that myself. For me, Provence is without fixed boundary posts. Each time I come to it its frontier with the northern world may be a little more north, a little more south, according to the way the spirit — and weather — moves me.

A perfect and spontaneous definition of Provence came from a young farmer with whom my wife and I fell into roadside conversation near Sablet in Vaucluse. "For us Provençaux", he said in the meridional accent which twangs like a released bowstring, "anything north of Montélimar is Siberia". It might have been Cézanne talking.

The traveller coming overland from the north knows he has entered Provence not so much by ascertaining his position on the map as sensing a climatic change. You drive along the valley road in Drôme, perhaps between Bourdeaux and Dieulefit, where, after a rainstorm weary clouds wrench themselves like a passing flock of sheep, leaving on the slate-grey rocks tattered tufts of wool. Or else the Roubion valley and Montagne de Couspeau, its backcloth, are suffused with golden spun-silk mist. As the road meanders south you realise you have slipped quietly into a firm, unambiguous landscape. A purity of light intensifies the natural colours, solidifies shapes, and sharpens the eyes for distant horizons. You are in Provence.

Northern Europe is behind you; Mediterranean Europe lies before, a fresh physical, climatic, biological and spiritual entity.

Provence is Mediterranean with a climate of hot, dry summers, temperate winters, and two periods of sustained rainfall in spring and autumn. A discontinuous but protective amphitheatre of mountains assures this climatic cycle. The most complete shelter — because it is the highest — is provided by the Maritime Alps which give the Côte d'Azur its sub-tropical vegetation and winter temperatures higher than anywhere else in France. Next come the Pre-Alps

Subtropical vegetation at Monaco

of Grasse and Digne. Then the long bald ridge of Lure, and Ventoux whose chalk pyramid slopes proud and solid into the alluvial plain of the Rhône, its head, botanically, in Lappland, its feet in the Mediterranean. On the far side of the river valley are the Vivarais and Cévennes ranges. Within these mountain barriers are lesser ridges. On the Riviera coast are two ancient stumps of eroded crystalline massifs, the Maures, and Estérel (once joined to the equally striking red rocks of Corsica). Many small limestone ridges run east and west — Lubéron, Alpilles, Ste. Victoire, Ste. Baume are some of the better-known names — which were folded under the waters of a once larger Mediterranean Sea; soft rocks squeezed into mineral waves when the harder masses of the Pyrenees and Alps were forming.

The protective amphitheatre is breached in the Rhône valley, to make it the Achilles' heel of the Provençal climate. Down the funnel rushes a chill wind off the cold uplands of central France, filling the void left by the rising thermals thrown up by the warm Mediterranean waters. This is the master-wind of Provence, the *mistral*. Sometimes ferocious in intensity, it can be penetratingly cold in winter. The massive farmhouses are fortresses against the wind; even with their blind north walls and roofs weighted with boulders they cannot keep out the piercing wind. It sears and dehydrates and, until the creation of a network of irrigation canals, prevented farmers from fully exploiting the fertile soil. Just as the winds of the eastern Mediterranean were woven into ancient Greek mythology, so the *mistral* has a Provençal mythology and literature all its own. In years gone by, it is said, if a man could prove he had committed murder during a *mistral* storm he was acquitted, so violently does the wind tear at the nerves.

Another vegetation heralds the entry into Mediterranean France. Gone are the lush meadows. Save on cool, moist, north-facing slopes, familiar northern plants and deciduous forests give way to evergreens — pines, evergreen oaks, pubescent oaks or cork oaks — and to stunted, thick-leaved, spiny, aromatic plants, all tough enough to withstand heat and drought. Cypresses and bamboos act as windbreaks. A stately cypress often stands on each side of the entrance gates to a property. They are known as Peace and Prosperity. Most characteristic tree of all is the olive, symbol of everything Mediterranean, of grace, gravity and moderation. Much of the landscape is treeless; the forests have been felled for thousands of years. Mediterranean man, I suspect, feels uncomfortable with too many trees pressed around him. Climate, erosion, burning and overgraz-

Hostile environment: sun, drought, salt in the Camargue

ing prevent easy regeneration. In Provence you are at the northernmost tip of the Sahara. Fugitive orchids or tall white asphodels flower briefly in spring on the heathlands or *garrigues*. Judas trees, orchards, golden wheat, scented broom and valerian on limestone hills, all give a burst of colour before the onset of high summer, which is the dormant period. Then, and until next spring, the vegetal mantle acquires a sage-green uniformity, while grasses and annuals wither to a leonine tawniness. In autumn, the crimson splashes of the vines are almost the only reminders of the northern leaf-change.

All plant and animal life has to find appropriate defences against insolation and drought. You do not have to be a botanist to see how shape, thickness and texture of wayside plants hint at the many devices nature uses in the battle for survival. Surprising though it may seem, this is a hostile environment. Even man has had, traditionally, to obey its laws, to use discretion.

This is the paradox of Provence. To imagine it as a land generous with warmth and light and harmony — a country of Cockaigne — is to misunderstand the essence of it. So much of the land is harsh and poor. This paradox gives depth and strength to its character and begins to explain why, for so many, Provence is an abiding passion.

What each person makes of Provence is a question of natural affinity, of temperamental response. We get on spontaneously with some people and not with others. Provence has all the complexities of a human character with its contradictions and shortcomings, its tender and harsh moods, its open and secretive traits. However spontaneously we may react to its sensory splendours there is no instant comprehension of Provence or the Provençaux even if they and we use the same brands of petrol and similar supermarkets.

I can think of no area of comparable size which has been so richly interpreted by painters, poets, writers and naturalists, but before their vision can be fully appreciated, one must have gauged Provence with one's own senses. Eye, ear, touch and smell give the first dimensions of the place. Above all, the eye. For the uncompromising light and atmospheric purity is unique in Europe, which is why the village of St. Michel near Forcalquier was chosen as the site for the French National Astrophysical Observatory. Five centuries of pictorial art have evolved in this light to culminate in Paul Cézanne who obsessively translated the architectural solidity and classical Mediterranean form through the agency of the Provençal light.

Never is this light more intense than when the *mistral* blows. All atmospheric moisture is dispersed and the eye perceives hitherto veiled details far away, and colours stand out crisp, solid and unalloyed. It is different on the coast. There, the air holds the moisture, and unstable marine reflections throw strange patterns. Colours become soft, rich, suggestive textures, as sensual as a September night by the sea. To the artist, maritime Provence is the 'Black Midi' which tempts him to paint the superficial in high-pitched colours. Some painters have been driven to despair, unable to find the inner restraint needed to withstand such stimuli.

Exaggerated responsiveness to this dazzling light is a real enough hazard for the northern artistic temperament. Vincent Van Gogh is the tragic and heroic example of a man over-excited and destroyed by the blinding southern light.

Self-protective restraint, almost in the biological way in which plants protect themselves from dehydration, must be set against over-responsiveness. Optically, objects are drained of their colour in that light; they are bleached to the muted greys and greens which dominate the natural vegetation.

If much of what we understand about the Provençal landscape is derived from artists, many of our misconceptions about the people of Provence have been formed by literature. Plays and novels have constructed stereotyped characters. The Provençal is loud, garrulous, boastful, exaggerating and gesturing; his nature is mercurial and childlike. He is lazy and unreliable. These identikit images may be drawn from the soufflé satires of the *Tartarin* books by Alphonse Daudet, a Provençal only by the accident of birth, or from Marcel Pagnol's trilogy of plays, *Marius*, *Fanny* and *César*, where humour is laced with pathos, as typically *Marseillais* and localised as is a Cockney to the east end of London. Or else from generations of writers from Britain who have perpetuated shallow myths about amusing natives. It is a patronising weakness to see natives as quaint and inferior.

From other literary sources emerges a Provençal who is so entranced by the tall tales he tells that he comes to believe them himself. Does this ebullient teller of yarns — *galéjades* — really exist? He is more symbolic then actual; he seems to me to stand for another type of man from the self-aware northerner who interprets character in terms of its inner components of conflict, guilt, absolution and self-conscious striving towards development. This is not an obsession in Provençal literature where personality is fixed and destiny is shaped by events.

There is a theatrical side to the Provençal which is nowhere better illustrated than when he is playing a game of *pétanque* on some rough patch of ground or in the village square. Accompanying each wristy throw and clink of metal ball against his opponent's is the gesture of suspense, of triumph, anguish or rebuke enacted with skill and artistry. An otherwise unspectacular game becomes a compressed drama of life. We glimpse the Provençal as passionate rather than emotional.

But I must avoid too much romantic generalisation. In terms of environment there are three distinct Provences which have bred differing characters. What they have had in common is the family smallholdings. In the past the proletarian and bourgeois ethos has been confined to the few large towns. The nobility and the peasant lived much the same kind of life, speaking the same language, feeling equal, behaving as equals and loving liberty. This was particularly so in the rich lowlands where everyone was fairly well off. The democratic, sociable Provençal belongs to the fat plains. His part of Provence has always been like a sponge absorbing every influence, every race to come by sea or down the Rhône, to make him tolerant, easy-going, adaptable.

A characteristic village: Puyméras in Vaucluse

The coast has produced different circumstances. Here, the fishermen have braved the sea and cultivated little plots of olives, figs, salads and bees, in order to subsist. For centuries the coast has been a magnet to the upland Provençaux and hill folk from further afield. These *gavots* (meaning people from around Gap) came down to find seasonal employment and, finding life easier, stayed. The littoral has always devoured the inland populations.

The Provençal of the hills inhabits the hard regions where the land is poor; there is little water and the crops are meagre. He has built the enclosed perched villages which contrast with the scattered farmsteads (or *mas*) of the fertile lowlands. Only in recent times has he found wealth from lavender cash crops which thrive on poor soil. His family life is more formal, patriarchal, slow, monosyllabic, withdrawn. He has been called a Cromwellian Roundhead without religion by the greatest of Provence's upland writers, Jean Giono. The archetypal figure of this region is Gaston Dominici, the peasant patriarch who was tried for the murder at Lurs of Sir Jack Drummond, his wife and daughter, in 1952.

A dignified restraint can be met with everywhere. These admirable traits are reflected in people's handshakes. Their hand remains inert in mine. I am reminded of a timorous animal lying passive and watchful in my palm. Is this not the outward sign of a natural aloofness? Even in friendship there must be reticence. I imagine Cézanne shaking hands like that.

The sense of reticence is imparted by the old hilltop villages. Narrow streets form a close arch of shade and secrecy. Thick walls and small windows cloak the privacy within, and speak of the suspicion of strangers. Peasants out in the mid-summer fields are thickly clothed against the hostile sun, just as the thick, rough trunks of the olive trees keep dark and cool the living sap within.

Of course, the youth of the countryside now strips to the waist as it works, and has learned sunworship from the northerner. Affluence has changed outlooks; mobility has withered yesterday's roots. The rich, imaginative and conserving mythology by which his grandfather lived is discarded. Yet you may still be confronted by a look of melancholy behind a man's eyes. As dusk throws its cool purple shroud over the landscape, a brief and chilling sense of isolation envelops me.

Perhaps I am falling back into the antique Mediterranean attitude, which even the hard-headed Romans held, that where the sun sets is the source of ill-fortune. Look to the east for renewal and good

Brantes dwarfed by the north flank of Mont Ventoux

The human scale: Chapelle St. Sixte, Eygalières

fortune. The main east-west Roman streets, the *decumana*, here in Provence as elsewhere, always saw the dead, and those condemned to death, leave by the ill-starred western gate.

The scale of the landscape seems to impose the scale of human values. Most landscapes in Provence are of human dimensions; there are no high alps to induce grandiose dreams. Each landscape has its own identity and nudges the mind towards thought and imagination which is moulded by that environment. The ideas that are swept into the head in the *mistral*-scourged Camargue differ from those of the Lubéron hills.

It has been the northerner with his inventive technology who has imposed ideas about taming nature. I suspect he has imported the urge to seek the spectacular and dramatic viewpoints, and is behind all those guidebook indications to the panoramic places. Is it perhaps a northern infantile fantasy of omnipotence to rush to the hilltops so as to survey everything at one's feet? I do not think this is the best way to get to know Provence. You must allow nature the upper hand; you must look up at her. The views from the top of Mont Ventoux are undeniably spectacular — as Petrarch, the first mountain-climbing tourist, recorded six hundred years ago — when the summit is not swathed in cloud. The real beauty of the mountain is in looking upward at its northern flank of strange pyramidal buttresses from the Toulourenc valley, or from the precariously balanced hamlet of Brantes. You must look upward to be aware of the majesty, proportion and structural stresses of Montagne Ste. Victoire, from the St. Antonin-sur-Bayon road, and see it as Cézanne did.

A remark by the Provençal painter, André Marchand, remains with me because I think it is valid. "It is not the sun which illuminates," he said, "but substances themselves which possess the power to illuminate". A short book can do no more than draw fleeting attention to a few of the substances that possess this power of illumination to those travellers in Provence who give them closer acquaintance.

2 · HISTORICAL PERSPECTIVES

A condensed historical survey can do no more than indicate the broadest trends and selected significant events. Where possible, I shall emphasise those that have left some visible trace in order to give reality to a million years of human activity in Provence.

Chipped stone artifacts in a cave at Roquebrune-Cap Martin on the Côte d'Azur have led some experts to date them from nearly a million years ago. Perhaps they were left by descendants of the first men to colonise Europe from Africa, crossing the Straits of Gibraltar and spreading along the warm and dry strip of the Mediterranean coast. These early men utilised caves and rock shelters and hunted the abundant wild animals. Later, Lower Palaeolithic men inhabited caves in Nice and Monaco, perhaps 70,000 to 125,000 years ago. Within one such cave, the Grotte du Lazaret, discovered in 1880, is a research laboratory and an exhibition room of finds, at 33 Boulevard Franck-Pilatte on the east side of Port Lympia in Nice. Similar sites have been located between Mont Ventoux and the Lubéron range; the little museum at Sault contains some of these early artifacts.

Best known of the prehistoric dwelling places are the Baoussé Roussé, the Red Rocks of Menton, occupied between 30,000 and 25,000 B.C. by the so-called Grimaldi 'negroid' and Cro-Magnon man. Skeletons in a contracted burial posture, dusted with red ochre and adorned with necklaces and bracelets of shells and fishbones have been unearthed. Some of the finds are in the museums of Menton and Monaco. With the skeletons were found fifteen female statuettes, some in stone, others in bone. They are similar to the 'Venus' statues of Périgord and elsewhere; the enlarged thighs and pregnant appearance suggest they may have been archaic mother-goddesses of a fertility cult. I do not know why, but Provence almost entirely lacks

Transhumance on foot, a vanishing tradition

the Aurignacian painted caves which are the glory of the Périgordian and Pyrenean caves.

Central Europe's glacial epochs never touched Provence directly, but with the retreat of the final glaciation between 10,000 and 8,000 B.C. the climate of Provence changed. There was less rain and water. Animals which Palaeolithic man had hunted retreated north. A less nomadic culture arose, the Mesolithic. In Provence Mesolithic man first domesticated wild sheep. By 5,000 to 4,000 B.C. he hunted, fished and evolved a pastoral life and made pottery. Later, in the Neolithic, he bred cattle and herded, grew cereal grasses and vegetable roots, modifying his stone tools as he exercised new skills. By late Neolithic times, as populations expanded, he devised techniques for building and creating settlements. The Grottes de Calès at Lamanon were inhabited uninterruptedly from the Neolithic to the 15th century. He also found that to protect his fixed territories he had to make war. Pre-Neolithic times had been almost a Garden of Eden in Provence.

Much of Neolithic culture remains in Provençal tradition. It was then that the *transhumance* began — the seasonal driving of sheep from the hot, shrivelling lowlands to the lush hill pastures. You will still see fields in June where flocks gather before being taken by lorry to the uplands; and they will return in October. In the Neolithic period the felling of the forests began for timber and fuel, for grazing and croplands, a process which has continued to our own times. Erosion has thinned the soil cover; the climate is too dry for easy spontaneous regeneration; goats have nibbled seedlings to prevent new forest growth. In the Neolithic period the first *drailles* were marked out, tracks used by shepherds and their flocks, and for centuries the subject of complex laws which reflected the hostility between nomadic shepherds and settled farmers. The tracks were used by traders in skins or salt; the Romans often merely enlarged them when constructing their roads. In the Neolithic period the first drystone, corbelled, round huts — *bories* — were built and continued to be built until the 17th century. Some 3,000 of them have been mapped round Gordes and Bonnieux in Vaucluse. Most are fairly recent restorations, but a few relics from the First and Second Iron Ages and Gallo-Roman times still lie recognisably about the stony plateaux.

The Bronze Age came to Provence about 2,000 B.C. Its most remarkable monument is at Mont Bégo, high in the Alpes-Maritimes, where some 46,000 carvings have been chipped on rock-faces exposed to the harsh elements — geometric figures, human figures, spears, hatchets and, most commonly, curved horns of cattle. Some of these petroglyphs may have been incised before the Bronze Age. Their meaning is enigmatic, as are the tribes that carved them.

They were probably a Ligurian tribe. The Ligurians, first mentioned in literature in the 6th century B.C., once occupied a large part of western Europe but were pressed back to coastal Provence and present-day Liguria (the Genoese Riviera) by the Celtic invasions which started in the 6th century B.C. The Ligurians created the first *oppida* — defensive positions or look-out posts behind drystone walls on high ground. One of the most interesting remaining examples is outside the tiny village of Chastellard-de-Lardiers, on the southern flank of Montagne de Lure. Originally a refuge, it later became a religious sanctuary from which a remarkable collection of offerings has been found.

We are beginning to step out of prehistory into history. Phoenician traders from Lebanon visited the Provençal coast about 1,000 B.C. They erected a temple in the 6th century B.C. to their god Herakles Monoikos, 'the sole divinity', and his name now survives only in Monaco, together with the legend that the demi-god passed through Provence from Spain to Italy, carrying the three golden apples from the Garden of the Hesperides. Greek Dorians from Rhodes settled on the coast. Celts infiltrated from inland and fused with the Ligurians. Phocaean Greeks came from near Izmir in Asia Minor to trade and then to found Marseille (*Massalia*) in 600 B.C. to create a conservative, aristocratic, commercial community, establishing trading posts along the coast. The early Greek remains of Antibes are in its museum at Bastion St. André. The Phocaeans introduced the Celto-Ligurians to money, raised their standard of living, and gave to the landscape of Provence two things we take for granted — the vine and the olive. At St. Blaise can be seen the best preserved Greek walls, close-fitted, mortarless blocks, still marked with assembly signs, that enclosed a military citadel.

From the 3rd century B.C., the religious and political capital of the Saluvii tribe which controlled the area between the Rhône, Durance and the sea, was the *oppidum* of Entremont, which can be visited, on a slope outside Aix-en-Provence. Its striking religious sculpture is housed at Musée Granet in Aix, and Musée Borély in Marseille.

In 218 B.C. Hannibal of Carthage marched his army and elephants through Provence (his route is fairly well known), paying Gallic chiefs handsomely for a peaceful passage on his way to attack Rome. Greek Marseille allied herself to Rome and helped to defeat the Carthaginians in the Punic Wars. *Massalia* helped Rome to ensure a safe overland route between Italy and newly acquired provinces in Spain. In return, the Romans aided Marseille, defeating the Saluvii in 124 B.C. They destroyed the *oppidum* of Entremont — where even now ballista balls hurled by the attackers lie about — and built the first Roman foundation, a *castellum*, where Aix now stands. Later, Marseille mistakenly sided with Pompey in his quarrel with Julius Caesar. Caesar forced Marseille into submission, building his engines of war out of the timber cut down from the sacred Gallic forest on La Ste-Baume. Marseille's power dwindled.

The story is now one of six centuries of Romanisation of Provence until the end of the Western Roman Empire in 476 A.D. A new Roman province, *Gallia Transalpina*, was carved out in 118 B.C. It reached from the Alps to the Pyrenees. Roman military might and organising genius brought peace and stability. An impressive example of meticulous efficiency is the marble cadastral plan in the museum at Orange — a surveyor's plan of all entitlements to property around *Arausio*, Roman Orange. Veteran Roman soldiers were settled and other colonies founded whose citizens acquired Latin rights. Magnificent and spacious public buildings are still preserved in cities such as Arles ('the little Rome of the Gauls'), Nîmes ('French Rome'), Orange, Glanum, Vaison ('the Pompeii of France') or Fréjus (founded by Julius Caesar). Communications were improved by a network of roads; vestiges of massive paving stones can be seen here and there, as well as bridges. The best-preserved is Pont Julien over the Coulon river near Apt, still able to bear modern traffic. Many a Roman milestone serves as an altar in churches up and down Provence. Roman arenas are put to the same uses today as 2,000 years ago. The bulls of the Camargue may well be descendants of those brought by the Romans to supply the bull-rings of *Provincia*. Trade flourished. There was political unity and economic expansion. Natives could acquire Roman citizenship or go to Rome and carve out a career. At her zenith Rome was tolerant of political and religious systems, provided they accepted Roman authority absolutely. Roman soldiers who had served in the east returned as worshippers of Mithras, the soldier sun god. A worn Roman bas-relief of Mithras can be seen just outside Bourg-St. Andéol, and St. Mitre-les-Remparts near the Etang de Berre is surely a Christianised form of Mithras. Submission to Roman authority is what the early Christians would not accept. For this reason alone were they persecuted. Local institutions were allowed to flourish. Ideally, *Provincia* was to reflect the character of Rome itself. In practice, there was excessive taxation and exaction; there were rapacious money-lenders and grasping governors. From time to time the natives rebelled.

Black bulls of the Camargue

An afternoon's harmless sport for boys and bulls

Under Julius Caesar's eight years of proconsular rule, Provence became a civil administration. In the Maritime Alps, where the loyalty of the Ligurians was uncertain, a military government was imposed. When these tribes were finally quelled the great Trophy of the Alps was erected by Augustus in 6 B.C. at La Turbie overlooking the sea, a fine monument to Roman power, authority and megalomania.

Christianity was introduced through Arles and Marseille. It appealed to the slaves, artisans and poorer city dwellers. Although it became the official faith of Rome with the conversion of Constantine the Great early in the 4th century, it spread slowly. Inland Provence was still in the process of being converted in the 16th century. What may be the oldest surviving Christian monument is a beautiful carved 2nd century sarcophagus in the small museum at Brignoles. The legend that a boatload of saints landed miraculously at Les

Ile St. Honorat, from the 4th century an influential religious centre

Saintes-Maries-de-la-Mer was sedulously cultivated and ensured the prosperity of an otherwise remote fishing village.

Even after the disintegration of the Western Roman Empire in the 5th century and the Burgundian and Visigoth occupation of Provence, Roman institutions endured.

Provence entered the Middle Ages under the Frankish (or Merovingian) kings. Their kingdom was unwieldy and Provence was left largely to its own devices and knew almost no peace for two centuries. There were invasions, rivalries and depopulation through epidemics. The country suffered more from Charles Martel who liberated it, than from the Arabs he evicted. At Venasque, the square baptistery with a low dome supported by columns is one of the few Merovingian buildings left from the 6th century.

Charlemagne reunited Provence fully into the Frankish kingdom and came to Apt in 776 to consecrate the church in whose upper crypt is a Carolingian altar. Saracenic invasions from the sea added to poverty and stagnation. In 884 A.D. they established a base at La Garde-Freinet in the Maures, raiding far and wide before being

Effigies of the two Marys at Les Saintes-Maries-de-la-Mer

driven away by William, Count of Provence. Little has endured of their presence. Some Arabic words have been absorbed into fishermen's language; the town of l'Almanarre derives from the Arab, Al Manar, lighthouse; some Saracen pottery; a few legends, one of which is that the ruined castle of Ste. Agnès near Menton was built by a Saracen prince converted to Christianity by the love of a local girl; in the Tour Ferrande at Pernes-les-Fontaines is a fresco of 1275 depicting a combat between a Moor and a Christian.

From William's victory emerged a strengthened feudal Provence.

Eze, medieval bastion against sea-borne invaders

Abandoned farms were revived and maritime commerce could be conducted in peace, yet famine and pestilence were never far away. Fatalistic despair expressed itself in the belief that the world would end in damnation in the year 1000. The world survived and the optimism bred from that fact, contributed to the First Crusade in 1095 in which a Provençal army distinguished itself in the Holy Land. Later St. Louis acquired the site of Aigues-Mortes from which to embark on the Crusade of 1248, and again in 1270. The splendid fortifications were built after his death.

Feuds and lawlessness — consequent on the Crusades — wracked the country. "The prisoner in his cell, the serf in his furrow, the monk in the cloister, and the lord in his castle" is how the historian Michelet summed up the Middle Ages. But this is a one-sided judgment. Through Provence lay the route of one of the three great medieval pilgrimages — to Santiago de Compostela — which began in the 11th century. Hospices and monasteries were erected by the monks of Cluny. Two of the most exquisite Romanesque (which the English call Norman) buildings on the pilgrims' route are the portals of St. Trophime in Arles and at St. Gilles. However unsettled the conditions, the pilgrimages continued.

In 1217 the greatest and most colourful fair in western Europe began at Beaucaire. It remained the magnet for merchants, entertainers, physicians and gypsies each July until the coming of the railways.

The hill villages which are so popular with visitors today — Eze, Gourdon, Roquebrune, Gilette and Sigale are but a few — were constructed in the Middle Ages. Built on the heights as protection from sea-borne invaders and from the malarious coast, these villages imposed a diminutive town existence on their inhabitants, a social pattern unchanged for centuries. Men went out to work in the fields to return at night. Life was intimate, closely knit, with everyone depending on everyone else for his special skills. It was ecologically efficient and determined the behaviour and outlook of the upland Provençaux ever since.

Provence in those days was famous for herbs. Monks and physicians came here to gather their simples; the Iles d'Hyères were particularly frequented. Go to any Provençal market today and see the many herbs for sale. Any well-run little hotel will provide a fresh herbal infusion. Herbs give the Provençal cuisine its distinction.

Medieval times were the breeding ground of imaginative, poetic folklore and creative traditions, only abandoned in recent years. It was the period of the troubadours, the lyrical poets who stressed the gentler, formal aspects of life — *la courtoisie*. They were mostly aristocrats who expressed their sentiments in Provençal, the *langue d'oc* which was — and is — the low Latin left behind by Roman soldiers and traders to be used by all peoples south of the Loire.

With the marriage in 1246 of Raymond-Bérenger V's daughter to Charles of Anjou who became Charles I of Provence, the country began to feel the influence of France. It almost turned away from its Mediterranean origins and looked north. Its architecture became northern Gothic; the Cistercians built Notre Dame du Bourg in Digne; the Dominicans began the basilica of St. Maximin. The church of St. Jean-de-Malte in Aix is completely French. Frenchmen were brought to the Provençal court as the troubadours' influence declined.

Provence was transformed from a comparative backwater, a mere corridor in European history, to the centre of events in 1309. The pope had been forced to flee Rome. He settled at Avignon where the Holy See owned the Comtat Venaissin. The huge fortified palace was built and five popes ruled there in the next seventy years. Avignon attracted wealth, prestige, artists and the intellectual élite. The presence of the popes protected overcrowded Avignon from outside disorder, piracy and intolerance. Shelter was given to Jews which is why there are synagogues at Carpentras and Cavaillon. Roving bands of Spaniards, Gascons and English — the indirect conse-

Tarascon castle guarding the Rhône

quences in Provence of the Hundred Years' War — had to be fought, and some semblance of peace returned with King René of Anjou who encouraged repopulation, agriculture, stockbreeding, navigation and the arts. He completed the handsome castle of Tarascon. His bulldog face appears in the *Buisson Ardent* triptych painted by Nicolas Froment, in the cathedral of St. Sauveur in Aix.

Formal union with France took place after Good King René's death in 1481, but some autonomy was left, although the Provençal language fell into decline when all judicial enactments had to be in French. Provençal names were Frenchified and incorrectly translated as place-names on maps. The Provençaux themselves showed their characteristic conservatism by resisting the artistic revival of the Renaissance. Medieval aspects were retained in the 16th century Hôtel de Ville in Arles, and in the châteaux of Gordes, Barroux and Lourmarin. The notorious predictions of Nostradamus of Salon, written in 1555, smack of medievalism, not of intellectual rebirth.

Religious views were strongly held, and Provence suffered cruelties similar to those of the Albigensian Crusade of the early 13th century, in Languedoc. A fundamentalist sect, the Vaudois, had settled in the Lubéron hills. In 1536 some members were convicted of heresy and burned at Aix, and later the inhabitants of a dozen villages were massacred. For years the hills were silent tombs. The ruins of Mérindol stand in mute testimony to those happenings, above the new village.

They presaged the Wars of Religion. Protestantism spread and flared into conflict for twenty years until in 1580 an outbreak of plague enfeebled the combatants. With Henri IV on the French throne a policy of pacification after so much fighting revived intellectual life in the province, and prosperity returned with Marseille as an economic capital, Aix an administrative one, Toulon as the naval port, and Avignon as a riverine port on the Rhône.

In 1635 the Thirty Years' War broke out. A Spanish fleet was put to flight by the people of St. Tropez on 15th June 1637, and on that day each year they celebrate the event with a colourful and noisy *bravade*, the Féte des Espagnols.

This was the century in which many fine public buildings were erected which can be seen today: the town halls of Marseille, Aix and Toulon — the latter famous because of the caryatids carved by the great Provençal sculptor, Pierre Puget — the colleges and seminaries of Carpentras, Avignon, Arles, and hospitals and theatres. The long aqueduct outside Carpentras belongs to this phase, as do many of the enchanting fountains, as in Aix and Pernes.

The maritime rivalry between England and France virtually began the close association between the British and the French Riviera. Nice and the territory east of the Var belonged to the Duke of Savoy in alliance with the British who attacked French Provence from the sea. Nice had a British consulate, and a number of British families lived there in a quarter known as Newborough — today the area round Place Croix de Marbre. Sir Henry Cavendish, the natural philosopher whose name is perpetuated through the Cavendish Laboratories at Cambridge, was born in Nice in 1731. At the end of the Seven Years' War (1756-63) Tobias Smollett undertook his journey to Nice for the sake of his health, staying there between 1763 and 1765. The publication of his letters, which are among the finest jewels of 18th century writing, are full of vigorous, biassed, penetrating and detailed accounts of life and customs, which brought the first visitors to the south of France. Like Smollett, they came in the hope of relief from lung tuberculosis. The real importance of Nice, Cannes, Menton and Hyères until the 1914-18 war was as curative centres for the 'white plague'.

Aix stands as the symbol of rising prosperity in the 17th and 18th centuries. It became an elegant provincial capital, and is still so, with the Cours Mirabeau shaded by huge plane trees, the Pavillon Vendôme, the many mansions or *hôtels*. Arts and science flourished; under benevolent royal despotism social life glittered. But the shadow of the Revolution was spreading.

The factors leading up to the French Revolution were complex social, material and moral tensions in which privilege, class, maladministration, greed and corruption played their parts. As elsewhere, disturbances in Provence coincided with high grain and bread prices.

Bravade at St. Tropez, the annual mid-June celebrations

The winter of 1788-9 was excessively cold; the harvest was bad. Discontent was widespread. Most Provençaux sided with the revolutionary cause; two powerful political figures represented them in the States General, the orator Mirabeau and the logician Abbé Sieyès. When in 1790, the Assembly decreed that France be divided into 83 *départements*, Abbé Sieyès wanted them to be equal squares; Mirabeau argued for boundaries that took into account custom, tradition, geography and language. He won the day. Provence was divided into three *départements* — Bouches-du-Rhône, Var and Basses-Alpes. In 1793 Vaucluse was added when papal ownership was given up, and the Alpes-Maritimes in 1860. Provence had become totally absorbed into France, and officially the name of the province had disappeared.

There was disorder and civil war in Provence. With the execution of the king in 1793 a sense of outrage gave rise to royalist sentiments, and at Toulon 'Louis XVII' was declared king and the rebels let in the Anglo-Spanish fleet in a war against the young Republic. This act scandalised France and young Captain Napoléon Bonaparte helped dislodge the English who had occupied Toulon.

Napoleon was never popular with either royalists or republicans in Provence. On his way to Elba he was almost assassinated at both Avignon and Orgon. On his return for the 100 Days escapade he landed at Golfe-Juan on 1st March 1815; the event is commemorated by a bust in a square of the town. Some Provençal towns hostile to him tried to capture him, so that his route from the coast was a fugitive one. Today's high road, the Route Napoléon (N85) is marked by imperial eagle milestones and plaques but it follows only short sections of the paths the Man of Destiny actually took. He went through wretched villages where he was either abused or overcharged. Near Digne, he handed five francs to an ill-kempt creature who cried, "Long live the Emperor! Down with Napoléon!" Not until Gap did he hear the first sweet music of acclaim. With the final collapse of the Empire, twelve Mameluks brought by Napoléon from Egypt were massacred by enraged Marseillais.

An economic paradox of the 19th century was that while industrial exploitation made use of new technologies, agriculture, the fundamental source of wealth for so much of Provence, remained static in its traditionalism. Towns were enlarged, roads improved, canals and bridges built. Bauxite was discovered at Les Baux in 1822 (today exploited in great quantities in the region round Brignoles). The handsome Roquefavour aqueduct near Aix was completed in

Grasse, capital of the perfume industry

1847; some have tried to see it as the modern Pont du Gard. Then came steam which revitalised the ports and brought the railways and the first of the tourists to the Côte d'Azur, and demanded coal which began to be scratched as lignite out of the ground at Gardanne. Small industries sprang up. There was brick-making at Aubagne, tanning at Barjols, soap-making at Marseille; the drab papermills still stand by the stream at Fontaine-de-Vaucluse. Traditional industries were modernised, in particular the perfume industry at Grasse. But wheat, olives, vines and sheep were losing out against cheaper imports, leading to the rural exodus, only halted in quite recent years.

Territorially, Provence remained untouched by the 1914-18 war, but the drain on its youth is signalled by each village monument and, not least, through one of the most impressive of all World War I novels — Jean Giono's *To the Slaughterhouse (Le Grand Troupeau* in the original French of 1931).

For better or worse, the transformation of Provence into modernity has taken place since then. Wheat, olives and sheep are in rapid decline (but not vines). Madder and silkworms are all but extinct. Now, early fruits, vegetables and cut-flowers are carried by rail, road and air for rapid export. Dams and power stations provide water and electricity to backward areas; even subalpine regions are coming to life again with sophisticated agricultural equipment. The oil installations of Lavéra and Fos, the nuclear research centre at Cadarache on the Durance, the Péchiney bauxite and aluminium transformers at Gardanne, or the cement works along the Rhône are far cry from romantic Provence. They are reminders, often ugly, of the price we pay for industrial wealth, but they are all part of the diverse realities of Provence.

For the Provençaux, the 1940-45 war meant defeat, occupation by Italians and Germans, aerial attacks by Allied aircraft, resistance and collaboration, and Franco-American landings on the coast and by airborne troops (La Motte was the first village to be liberated). At Le Drammont stands the memorial to the American landing of 15th August, 1944; at Boulouris is the cemetery of the French who died during the same landing; the National Memorial to the Landings in Provence is in Tour Beaumont high on Mont Faron behind Toulon. Wayside tablets mutely remember those who were shot by the Germans, and other episodes of a bitter past.

Here and there are architecturally incongruous monuments to recent colonial history which has drawn Algerians and Indochinese to work in France. At Aubagne are the headquarters and museum of the French Foreign Legion. Outside Fréjus are a Buddhist pagoda built by Indochinese in 1914-18, an Annamite cemetery, and the Missiri Sudanese mosque.

The tourist may not be much concerned with the Péchiney company's wish to erect a factory in the Alpilles; or with the military uses to which the Plateau d'Albion and Plan de Canjuers are put; with the growth of cementscapes along the coast (unless he knew it years ago); or with the expansion needed by the company producing chemicals in the Camargue saltings. These conflicts of environmental interests are universal. Reflective travellers will find their affinity with old villages where old men, immobile, black-vested, sit beneath the plane trees. They seem like Henry Moore figures, withdrawn, contemplating the hubbub about them — the embodiment of timeless Provence with which the following chapters are also more concerned.

3 · APPROACH FROM THE NORTH: THE RHÔNE VALLEY AND TRICASTIN

Each road into Provence offers its own prospects. The one I propose to make use of now travels down from fairly far north, running near enough parallel to the A7 autoroute which the whole world takes in midsummer, yet just far enough away from the congested Rhône. It is a homely country road, discreet and obedient to contours, and is the N538 which links the 250 kilometres between Vienne and Cavaillon. It passes through no large towns; it crosses rivers thirsting to get to the Rhône; it climbs a few hills, and keeps the graceful Dauphiné foothills as an eastern backcloth. It allows you to stop and invites you to look. It has some quite beautiful picnic places; one of them, outside Bourdeaux, my wife and I have appropriated over the years and it is balm to the senses. Ten kilometres beyond it is Dieulefit coming close to the northern fringe of Provence. At a corner of Place Châteauras, which is little more than a bulge in the main street, is the Grand-Hôtel du Levant, modern and well appointed, where a night's stay is agreeable and inexpensive.

A general comment, at this point, about hotels. Those I mention have added to the sum of our pleasure. Not that they have been perfect, but any shortcomings have been redeemed by some other gratefully remembered quality. Some have been visited recently; others we have not been to for some years and comments about them may be out-of-date. It is best to consult two publications which are revised annually. One is the *Guide Michelin*; its thoughts may not be infallible, but it is an indispensable little red book to carry through the length and breadth of France. The other is the *Guide des Logis de France*, a directory of mostly small, unpretentious hotels in rural areas and small towns, often inexpensive, usually reliable. Naturally, there is some overlap between the two guides.

Small, family-run hotels impart an atmosphere of intimacy. In

Harvesting grapes near the Var coast

return, the guest must make every effort to speak French, and not expect invariable graciousness from the *patron*. You must take the French as they are. An occasional prickly disobligingness (which means no more than an anxious preoccupation with some other matter) can be dissolved to solicitous concern by a patient and sympathetic word. Heel-digging is a counter-productive posture. The hotels we have stayed at have charged modestly, or at least we have not begrudged the bill. You may still chance upon Provençal hotels which greet the visitor with a smell of beeswax polish on sparkling red hexagonal tiles; with lavender in wardrobes with the traditional spiral-moulding design; and where beds are covered with quilts of glowing red, green and yellow Provençal patterns. They should be savoured, for they are rarer now.

Olive oil, garlic and herbs are the staples of taste, smell and vigour in Provençal dishes. Famous regional dishes with diverse scarce ingredients take a long time to prepare and are incompatible with a low-priced menu. Prestigious recipes for *bouillabaisse* (a stew of a

41

variety of expensive Mediterranean fish flavoured with garlic and saffron), for which every restaurant has *the* authentic contents; or the subtler *bourride*; or *brandade de morue* (pounded salt cod with cream, olive oil and garlic); or *loup de mer* (sea-bass grilled over burning fennel); all these should be reverenced at prestigious restaurants. You pay accordingly. *Guide Michelin* will tell you where they are, and Provence has some superlative restaurants.

On many middle-priced menus are Provençal specialities, such as *filet de porc* marinaded in wine, herbs and garlic; red mullet; Provençal tripe; *tapenade*, an hors d'oeuvres of pounded olives, anchovies, tuna fish and capers to make a dark, shining paste; tomatoes grilled with garlic and breadcrumbs and olive oil; the unctuous garlic mayonnaise called *aioli*. Around Nice are many good things typical of the region, of which *ratatouille*, *pissaladière* and *salade niçoise* have become known everywhere. The best sea-foods are on the coast. The Camargue speciality is *riz de Camargue*, a sea-food risotto, and Camargue beef.

As to wine, outside Châteauneuf-du-Pape, Girondas, and Travel rosé from just across the Rhône, there are few easily available, distinguished wines. *Côtes de Provence* are the mediocre wines of the Riviera. But particularly in Vaucluse, restaurant wine-lists will have interesting local wines, the *vins du pays*. Each district, each village even, has its vintage which never travels far and never gets a mention in the wine books. With a little practice taste-buds begin to pick out and remember their 'unknown' favourites.

Which brings me back to the Grand-Hôtel du Levant at Dieulefit. You eat well and inexpensively in its large and handsome dining room. Try its Visan rosé, from the village of that name further south. It is dry, tingles faintly on the palate, and goes gaily and briefly to the head.

South of Dieulefit the N538 runs mostly downhill. After thirteen kilometres, with the Nyons hills ahead and a plain away to the west, a right turn (D14) signposts Taulignan and Grignan. You are entering Tricastin, a small, triangular district which is called by the subtle and almost untranslatable word *pays*. Tricastin has no administrative significance, only a distant historical one. The *pays* lies inside a triangle formed by Montélimar, Nyons and Orange. Its slight hills of limestone and sandstone ripple from the Dauphiné mountains to the banks of the Rhône to form a geographical enclave a little to one side of main routes and tourist magnets. Once madder was an important dye-crop; now, the plains are intensively cultivated with vines, fodder crops, market-garden produce and tobacco, wherever irrigation canals exist. Tricastin is only slightly modified from the name by which the Romans knew it, the territory of the Tricastini tribe, crossed by Hannibal in 218 B.C.

Taulignan is the prototype of many villages hereabouts. Remnants of old ramparts, fortified gateways, towers and houses enclosing a circular promenade — a *cours* — shaded by plane trees can be repeated with variations. Some are larger, some smaller, but they cling to their pinnacles, supporting ruined castles or donjons or medieval walls with an air of resignation. All were once feudal or Renaissance domains. Valréas is the largest town in Tricastin. St. Paul-Trois-Châteaux was the capital of the Tricastini. Chamaret, La Baume-de-Transit, Chantemerle-lès-Grignan, Richerenches all present a different profile. Suze-la-Rousse has an imposing château above the river Lez, 800 years ago the property of the Princes of Orange.

Outside Montségur-sur-Lauzon is Solérieux where lies the Ferme St. Michel, once a beautiful and sturdy farm or *mas*, now a hotel standing alone in the deep Tricastin countryside, a centre from which to roam the network of unsignposted lanes. Take care when you use the hotel's swimming pool. It has (or had) no handrail, nor steps; although I am well over six feet I was submerged at the shallow end!

Grignan, ten kilometres west of Taulignan is the main tourist attraction on account of a somewhat overpowering Renaissance château, a place of literary pilgrimage by those who admire the witty and observant letters by Madame de Sévigné to her daughter, sometimes written from the château. Madame de Sévigné died at Grignan in 1696.

Head west and keep the village of Vallaurie on your right. A little beyond it a narrow road (D133) turns left and brings you in about six kilometres to an unexpected and romantic place. Beneath the trees a brook babbles, and to the left of the road are the soberly beautiful remains of an 11th century Romanesque building, Chapelle du Val des Nymphes. Its apse, open to the sky, has one colonnade of arches immediately above another below the half-cupola of the apsidal vault. Certainly, a pre-Christian, pagan temple must have stood here earlier, for this is just the sort of poetic spot at which the Gauls worshipped their water deities.

A little further on the road rises to the partly ruined village of La Garde-Adhémar. Its church has a most unusual feature. It has an

43

apse at each end. I am never quite able to reconcile my eye to an appreciation of the stiff belfry architecture which is characteristic of much of the Romanesque style. From the ramparts are views across the wide Rhône valley to the Vivarais hills. Below, is the twenty-eight kilometre long Canal de Donzère-Mondragon which diverts a substantial quantity of water from the Rhône for both navigational as well as hydro-electrical purposes. Cutting a similarly straight swathe is the parallel A7 autoroute, and almost equally parallel to them both is the old road from Bollène. It all looks very efficient, very Roman. And the little road (D158) south from La Garde-Adhémar to St. Paul-Trois-Châteaux is probably the modern top-covering of the Roman highway between Arles and Lyon, the *Via Agrippa*. St. Paul-Trois-Chateaux (it has never had three castles), capital of the Tricastini tribe and *Augusta Tricastinorum* under Emperor Augustus, contains much to delay the traveller — medieval, tortuous streets, Renaissance houses, and a 12th century church. It was once a cathedral, and the proportions, decorative details and mosaic pavings make this a particularly harmonious building. It is unusual in Provence to find a nave lit by windows.

A little deviation off the Suze-la-Rousse road (D59) goes to one of the most charming of the Tricastin villages, St. Restitut on the edge of a limestone plateau. In this cheerful and colourful place the 12th century church is richly decorated. Half way up the funerary tower beside it are bas-reliefs of the signs of the Zodiac, of Adam, Eve, the three Magi, real and symbolic animals which may represent the ancient monster myths which abound in western Provence. Some people are convinced that this tower stands over the tomb of St. Restitut, first bishop of St. Paul-Trois-Châteaux, whose blindness Jesus is said to have cured.

The direct road through Suze-la-Rousse passes through the delightfully named Ste. Cécile-les-Vignes just in Vaucluse from Drôme. Far across the flat land, where the heat of summer silences everything except the cicadas, rises the hump of Mont Ventoux and the abrupt needles of the Dentelles de Montmirail. A little further on is Sérignan-du-Comtat, a village preoccupied with producing wine. Near its bulky, fortified church is a statue of the naturalist, Jean-Henri Fabre (1823-1915), seated, peering at some small creature through his hand-lens, wearing the large, floppy hat of felt which accompanied him on his rambles. His house where he wrote his books on natural history, now a museum, is just outside the village on the Orange road.

It is not merely my own bias towards the natural history of Provence that directs this chapter's steps to Sérignan. The English translations of Fabre's works gave to an older generation a clear, poetic, yet objective insight into the lives of southern insects, and made a corner of Provence almost familiar to many who never set foot in it. Fabre's style, a mixture of Virgil, Gilbert White and Charles Darwin, is too discursive, too anecdotal and homely for the science student of today. Convictions of faith made Fabre reject evolution by natural selection — Darwin admired him nonetheless — and so in our eyes his scientific credentials seem limited. Fabre's genius lay in uniting religion and observation, poetry (he was an accomplished poet in Provençal and a friend of Mistral) with art (his paintings of mushrooms in the museum reveal his delicate skill). His passionate search for truth in nature was of the same order as Cézanne's. The *Souvenirs Entomologiques* were written a century ago and still illuminate Provence through the lives of the wasps, spiders, glow-worms, cicadas, mantids and grasshoppers.

When I first visited the museum, Fabre's son was still curator; his presence rolled back the years to when *Moussu Fabré* laboured there from 1879 until his death in 1915. His name was honoured round the world but his life had never been far from the peasant poverty of his childhood in Aveyron. A look at the manuscripts on which the old man had worked shows a handwriting which traces gently swelling bulges across the sheet, an insistant rhythm of parallel curves.

Whether the Sérignan of 2,000 years ago resounded to the trumpetings of Hannibal's thirty-seven elephants, no-one knows, but they did cross the Aygues just south of the village. Our route does the same to get to Orange by way of Camaret whose medieval walls and fortified gateways and wrought-iron belfry compel the camera.

By what curious twists of history did Orange become linked with England? The counts of Orange (the name a distortion of *Arausio* as the town was known under the Romans) were created by Charlemagne; by the 13th century it had made itself a principality and through inter-marriage became part of the possessions of William of Nassau when he became William III of England in 1688. In his war against Louis XIV, the French occupied Orange and destroyed the defensive walls and citadel. William got it back again at the Treaty of Ryswick in 1697. On his death Orange was inherited by the King of Prussia who gave it to France in 1713 while retaining the title for a piece of Dutch Gelderland, surviving in the Netherlands' royal House of Orange.

Orange, a performance in the floodlit Roman theatre

The arch and the theatre are the two chief monuments, and both are impressive remains of the Roman city of *Arausio*, settled by veterans of the Second Legion, and previously the capital of the Celtic Cavares. At the height of its Roman prosperity its population numbered 100,000; today it is less than 26,000. It had been endowed with all the fine and essential buildings of a Roman city, but most were destroyed in 412 A.D. when the Visigoths overran Orange. Near the theatre mere fragments of a gymnasium, portico, temple, plus three more temples which had formed part of the Roman capitol on the hill of St. Eutrope, remain.

Louis XIV said of the theatre facade that it was the finest wall in his kingdom. From the outside, the massive blank wall shows two rows of projecting sockets high above the blind arcade; these supported the poles from which the *velarium* or sun-blind was suspended over the auditorium. On the opposite side everything is more elaborate. The huge statue of Augustus, in whose reign the theatre was erected, has been restored from fragments. At his foot is a kneeling Gaul, pleading for mercy, an emphatic reminder of imperial supremacy. In its heyday, the facade was ornamented with many columns, statues, marbles, mosaics and friezes of figures from Greek tragedy. In front of the stage is the rectangular pit which housed sophisticated machinery for changing the scenery. Parallel to the pit is a slot from which the interval curtain was raised. A few rows of seats have been restored to hold 7,000; once the auditorium could seat some 11,000 spectators. The acoustics remain splendid.

The theatre can be viewed in comparative peace. Not so the triumphal arch which stands four-square in the middle of N7, forcing traffic along a roundabout. In the early morning out of season there is a better chance of careful contemplation. It is a matter of amazement to me that this large and richly decorated arch is so well preserved, considering the erosion thrust on it by 2,000 years of buffeting by the *mistral* wind. Only the western face has been restored. Here is triumphant imperial Rome proclaiming the valour and victories of the Second Legion. Every space seems to be crammed with carvings: trophies, insignia, inscriptions, shields, battle standards, and the double Capricorn which was the insignia of the Second Legion and the zodiacal sign of Augustus himself. There are friezes of victorious Roman infantry and cavalry fighting naked barbarians who are, of course, being worsted, and chained prisoners — a revelling in triumphant, even arrogant carnage. On the east side are six large figures of defeated Gallic leaders. One wonders what thoughts passed through

Orange, the splendidly preserved Roman arch

the minds of the Gallic craftsmen — presumably — who carved them.

High over the two smaller arches on the north flank are perhaps the most remarkable reliefs of all. They represent naval spoils, and this is the largest known collection of them. Remarkable because the Romans were undistinguished sailors with no great liking for the sea. Perhaps these reliefs commemorate Caesar's naval victory over the Gallo-Greek forces off Marseille in 49 B.C. Or all these carvings of galleys, tridents, prows, masts, anchors and more besides may celebrate Octavian's victory over Antony and Cleopatra at Actium in 31 B.C. Once the arch had supported a bronze figure of Tiberius, emperor between 14 and 37 A.D., in a chariot drawn by four horses.

The Musée Municipal is almost opposite the theatre and is worth visiting to see the fragments of the cadastral plan which I mentioned in Chapter II, for few remnants surviving from Roman times give such startlingly clear insight into Roman efficiency and respect for legal minutiae. This plan of *Arausio* was engraved on a huge sheet of marble in 77 A.D. on the orders of Emperor Vespasian for display in a public building. Unearthed in 1949, this cadastral plan indicated the configuration of the land; the surveyor's grid was scaled to *centuria* (a unit of 710 metres square) into which the land was divided. It surveyed all the farms; the entitlement to property. It was the official record of ownership for taxation purposes of both the veteran Roman legionaries as well as the local Cavares people who received the poorest land. Unpaid taxes were subjected to a six per cent. interest rate. Aerial photography has shown how some parts of the cadastral plan correspond to still traceable boundaries.

From near the theatre a secondary road (D68) goes under the autoroute and on to Châteauneuf-du-Pape, delightfully surrounded by its celebrated vineyards, the ruins of a castle built as a summer palace by the popes at Avignon, keeping watch over the village. Then Sorgues and the busy road into Avignon.

If the interest in Orange is mainly Roman, Avignon is medieval in the shape of the vast, grim fortress of the Palace of the Popes and the ramparts they threw round their Rome-in-exile. It can only be visited at fixed times and with conducted parties, and is a labyrinth of halls, apartment rooms, corridors, courtyards, towers and chapels. A few paintings bring reminders of a gentler life.

The most influential painter to be brought to Avignon was Simone Martini from Siena who worked in Avignon between 1340 and 1344, and all that remains of his work in Provence are the fres-

Avignon, Palace of the Popes and the Rhône

coes in poor condition in the Salle des Festins, which were removed in 1962 from the porch of the cathedral of Notre Dame des Doms. Matteo Giovanetti followed him, and the decorative themes of trees, flowers, bathers, huntsmen and falconers with stags or fish in a number of towers and chapels in the Palace are attributed to him. Both these Italian painters showed how paint could be used to cover large surfaces, replacing the traditional miniatures and tapestry work, and how space could be filled with natural scenes. Under Giovanetti fresco artists were imported from Spain, France, England, Germany and the Low Countries for a School of Avignon to become established.

There is much besides to see: the cathedral, numerous churches, the picturesque Pont St. Bénézet with only four arches and a chapel remaining; the old quarters are extensive and attractive with 17th century mansions, and Rue des Teinturiers (Dyers' Row) with some old water-wheels silent above the flow of the Sorgue is perhaps the most walk-worthy of all; the museums are full of fascination.

Or, as a rest from sightseeing, the gardens of Rocher des Doms look over the river Rhône, and the streets and shops and restaurants seem forever bursting with vigour. Across the river, Villeneuve-lès-Avignon offers its handsome tower of Philippe le Bel and Fort St. André. The Charterhouse of Val de Bénédiction has more frescoes by Matteo Giovanetti; the church of Notre Dame has a 14th century polychrome ivory of the Madonna carved from an elephant's tusk. At the Musée de l'Hospice is the remarkable picture in oil by Enguerrand Quarton, painted in 1453-4, *Couronnement de la Vierge*, one of the first paintings to include a recognisable landscape. Here you can make out Mont Ventoux as well as some fjords or *calanques* near Marseille.

For a few days of sightseeing I prefer to stay at Villeneuve rather than in congested Avignon. Hôtel l'Atelier, 5 Rue de la Foire, near the museum, is a gracious 16th century house which, unfortunately, no longer has a restaurant.

4·BASTION OF THE ALPS: AROUND MONT VENTOUX

In the last chapter the itinerary turned from the N538 after Dieulefit to look at the Tricastin *pays*. By now continuing south along it towards Nyons, you come to Le Pégue, a little way off the main road. Some of the honey-coloured houses have bits of Roman masonry embedded in their walls, a hint that there is something archaeological afoot. Layers of superimposed settlements from the Bronze Age on have been uncovered. What has surprised the experts is the evidence of a deeper northward penetration by the Greeks of Marseille between the 6th and 2nd centuries B.C. than had been supposed. Some of the finds can be seen at the little archaeological museum in the village.

Nyons on the Aygues is popular with French families in summer and there are numerous hotels in this sprightly resort. Hôtel Colombet, on one side of the arcaded Place de la Libération, is fairly large (34 bedrooms), efficient and not to be faulted for a night's stop. For a settled base I would choose Mirabel-aux-Baronnies, seven kilometres further on. Hôtel Mirabeau is an elegant old house on the edge of the village; there are only eight bedrooms, furnished in traditional Provençal style, and it has a large panelled restaurant. Some rooms look out over the small garden towards quiet slopes beyond. One of the best local red wines is Vinsobres.

Just south of Nyons are the first olive groves whose trees grow good black olives. Northeast runs the road to Serre, 64 kilometres away in Hautes-Alpes, through strangely bare hills whose folds are brought to a textured glow and brilliance by a slanting evening sun. South of this road is an area of quiet byways, somnolent hamlets, where the largest town's population can be counted in hundreds, and few inns come to the notice of the guidebooks. A lost, attractive corner, well worth a visit.

Vaison-la-Romaine and the excavations

South from Nyons or Mirabel to Vaison-la-Romaine is a busier route. Vaison, on one side of the river Ouvèze, is medieval. On the other, and joined to it by the original single-span Roman bridge, are Roman and modern Vaison. The antiquities are the attraction. Their background is the pyramid of Mont Ventoux, *Mons Ventuosus*, the Windy Mountain, the "mirror of the eagles", as the Provençal poet, René Char has expressed it. In the ruins, the scale is human, unlike the grandiosity of Orange, Nîmes or Arles. True, there is the reconstructed theatre, but one walks past the modest houses, shops and workshops of Celts, Ligurians, Greeks and Romans, as well as the finer properties of the aristocracy. There is even a five-seater privy. *Vasio Vocontiorum* represents the good life to be destroyed by the

5th century barbarian invasions. Vaison is a small-scale Pompeii. Among the many statues one of the finest is only a copy. The original is in London. It is of Diadumenos (a boy binding his hair). Unearthed in 1862 and swopped for a box of silkworm cocoons, the owner tried to sell the treasure to the Louvre, but the officials did not care for his politics. So he offered it to the British Museum which acquired a bargain.

Hotels in Vaison are not outstanding, but the Hôtel Théâtre Romain, Place Chanoine-Sautel, is functionally adequate for an overnight stop by archaeological enthusiasts.

Mont Ventoux dominates the landscape. It is close on 2,000 metres (6,000 ft) high though its bulk makes it look less. For a comprehensive view of it go a couple of kilometres out of Malaucène on the Beaumes-de-Venise road. Now you see it in its proper setting among the smaller, comically tilted Baronnies hills, its bald pate dusted with chalk which has passed as snow for many a passer-by. The motor-road winds to the top for twenty-one kilometres from Malaucène, a town of character, history, and immense plane trees. First the road goes through the plantations of trees, only begun in 1860, then across the stony wastes whose sparse grasses give bare nourishment to flocks of sheep.

Most people go to the top for the views. It is all quite easy, and often congested. The road is used for motor-racing, and sometimes for the Tour de France cycle race. In winter the slopes are the preserve of skiers. It was different once. A plaque amid the hotels, observatory, television station and Air Force installation, says that the poet Petrarch climbed Mont Ventoux in the spring of 1336. That was an expedition demanding moral and physical courage. Ever since his school days in Carpentras Petrarch had dreamed of making the ascent. Others had been obliged to climb mountains before him. He became the first man to climb out of sheer curiosity and the wish to meet a natural challenge for its own sake. He recorded the adventure in a letter to his spiritual adviser.

He and his brother left Malaucène in late April 1336. It was an exhausting and terrifying ordeal. By this act he broke with medieval humility and submissiveness to both nature and God. Almost the first man, one might say, who began to measure things by men, a humanist. He has been called the first modern man, a Renaissance man whose outlook and character are familiar to us. Critical, vain, adventurous, restless, politically adroit, filled with curiosity for natural science, he was an individualist. He was something of a hypocrite and not entirely likeable but, oddly, there went the first modern tourist, exploring in Provence.

A circuit round the base of the long east-west crest of Mont Ventoux is a journey from a northern to a southern landscape, from *ubac* to *adret* as they say in Provençal. From the general direction of Vaison you make for Mollans-sur-Ouvèze and D40 which later rises to follow the sourceward course of the poplar-lined Toulourenc. On the right the immense flank of Ventoux, buttressed by purple, yellow and grey pyramidal *molasses* or deposits which have slipped down the steep slopes, almost shuts out the sky. Dark conifers cling to the mountain's sides. You pass one or two villages. St. Léger-du-Ventoux is the starting point for the climb up Ventoux, and further on, Brantes, precariously balanced on its rock, looks up towards Ventoux's highest point, and in June pickers gather the flowers from the small lime trees. At Reilhanette the road swings south where Ventoux ends, for Sault-de-Vaucluse, though it would be almost equally delightful to go straight on to the N85 and Sisteron by following the completely rural Jabron valley.

The name of Sault stems from low latin, *saltus*, referring to the partly wooded grazing ground which once existed and has been destroyed by clearing, burning and over-grazing. To the northeast of Sault rise the southern and gentler slopes of Ventoux. In the opposite direction is the huge Plateau de Vaucluse into whose fissured limestone soil rain seeps and gathers in the hundreds of subterranean caves or *avens* — especially round St. Christol — to drain by invisible streams and surge out at Fontaine de Vaucluse, perhaps thirty kilometres to the southwest. The Plateau de St. Christol has the melancholy distinction of housing atomic weapon silos.

The Sault to Carpentras road (N524) plunges deep and winding through the Gorges de la Nesque to emerge at Villes-sur-Auzon. Next is Mazan. At the approach to the village is its cemetery on a knoll. Riding on top of the boundary wall, and surrounded by cypresses, are sixty-one well-preserved Gallo-Roman sarcophagi. The far more famous ones in the Alyscamps of Arles are in much more cramped and noisy conditions than here. Also in the cemetery is a half-buried chapel, Notre Dame de Pareloup, literally Our Lady of Protection against Wolves. This chapel was built in the 11th and 12th centuries and rebuilt in the 17th century, to exorcise the demons which came in animal guise to devour the dead in the graves, which they actually did in the real form of wolves.

All sorts of interesting digressions can be made from Mazan.

Fontaine de Vaucluse and the resurgent river Sorgue

A parched country, yet every village has its fountain: Vence

There are villages like Mormoiron on a limestone spur, or Caromb, which like so many other Provençal villages, boasts a wrought-iron belfry. The bell is open to the sky, a large and ornate *sonnaille* or goat-bell. At the fountain grotesque carved masks spout water. How strange, I often reflect, that every village has cool, copious fountains that never stop, in such an arid land where, not long ago, they used regularly to pray for rain.

North of Mazan lies Bédoin. By turning left on to the D19 in Bédoin you come in about two kilometres to an easily overlooked entrance to a farmyard on the left. Just inside, and hidden by a belt of trees, is one of the most attractive country chapels I know — La Madeleine. From the yard you face three neat semi-circular apses clinging one against the other, like house-martins' nests, to the wall of the chapel. From the middle of the wall rises a square tower whose severe facade is pierced by small rounded windows on three levels, and topped by the mere skull-cap of a dome. Ancient, weather-beaten tiles cover roof, apses and dome. Forming a distant background are the sharp tips of the Dentelles de Montmirail.

South of Mazan is the particularly handsome perched village of Venasque, the support walls in part made of Roman bricks. It was once *Venasca* which gave its name to the Comtat Venaissin. Between the 6th and 10th centuries it was the seat of the bishops of Carpentras, which is why it has one of the few Merovingian buildings in Provence. This is the 6th century baptistery, restored in the 12th century, possibly built over an earlier temple to Venus. It is square with an apse on each side, and the dome is supported by graceful pink and white marble columns. At the foot of Venasque is another Merovingian chapel, Notre Dame de la Vie which contains the tomb of Boethius, bishop of Venasque-Carpentras, who died in 604.

To get to Carpentras from Venasque by Pernes-les-Fontaines is, admittedly, a detour but it would not be in vain. Pernes, in fruit-growing country, is graced by thirty-two fountains in its streets and squares. The most charming is Fontaine du Cormoran (or Cormorant) of the 17th century in the Rue Raspail. What may be the oldest surviving frescoes in Provence are on the upper walls inside the 13th century Tour Ferrande in the Quai de Verdun. Although not as elegantly painted as the frescoes in the Papal Palace of Avignon, those at Pernes, painted around 1275, are factually informative, realistic and perkily witty in execution. There is, for instance, a representation of Pope Clement IV investing Charles of Anjou with the Kingdom of Naples in 1266, and an amusingly fierce combat on horseback between a Christian and a Moor.

Six kilometres to the north is Carpentras, capital of the Comtat Venaissin until the French Revolution, well known for its candied fruits, honey from the slopes of Mont Ventoux (which is said to rival the honey of Hymettus), and its *berlingots*. I suppose we would call these bullseyes, but I suspect they will disappoint the sweet-toothed specialists from England.

The antiquity of Carpentras is testified by the municipal arch built about the same time as the arch at Orange, perhaps during the reign of Tiberius, and commemorating Augustus's victories in Germany and the East. Again the theme of chained captives. On the east face, one of the better dressed figures could be that of the nobleman Sacrovir who led an unsuccessful rising against crippling taxation and brutal Roman government in 21 A.D. Carpentras then was *Carpentoracte Meminorum*, capital of the Meminian Gauls; the root of the name lies in the Celtic *karpenton*, a two-wheeled cart drawn by two horses. The arch stands in the courtyard of the Palais de Justice of the 17th century. Close by is the former cathedral, the church of St. Siffrein (a mysterious patron saint of Carpentras who appears in no hagiography), late Gothic, with a Flamboyant south porch. Inside are works by the 17th century sculptor from Mazan, Jacques Bernus whose fame was surpassed only by Pierre Puget's. Beyond the vaulted sacristy are the remains of the original Romanesque church. Outside again, in the triangular ogee above the Jewish Door is carved a globe being gnawed by rats, the *Boule aux Rats*. What this signifies has given rise to the wildest of speculations. The writer J.P. Clébert advances a factual interpretation. The rats signify, he says, what they were, plague and typhus carriers into Provence and Europe generally, where they had been unknown before the 12th century, having been brought back by Crusaders from the Holy Land. The carving of the 15th century can be seen, therefore, as an exorcism of the pestilence sent by divine wrath at human sinfulness.

The importance of Carpentras as a capital until the 18th century is reflected in the Hôtel-Dieu or hospital, built with delightful Rococo ebullience by Bishop d'Inguimbert whose tomb is inside the building. Another interesting sight is the oldest synagogue in France, founded in the 14th century, rebuilt in the 17th century. In the old foundations is the *cabussadou*, the ritual purification bath for young girls on the eve of their marriage.

Of the four museums, Musée Comtadin in Boulevard Albin, contains local ethnological exhibits, including a collection of *sonnailles* or bells used in the seasonal movement of sheep, the *transhumance*. From the 18th century on they have been made by Simon of Carpentras, father and son, for all the shepherds of Provence and even further afield. Each type of bell has its own Provençal name, and there are dozens of them. The collective sound of each flock had to be distinctive, and all the bells in one flock were made to be in complete musical harmony. The generations of Simons of Carpentras were all musicians, too.

Dentelles de Montmirail and Mont Ventoux beyond

Notre Dame d'Aubune near Beaumes-de-Venise (Vaucluse)

A few kilometres north of Carpentras are the Dentelles de Montmirail. Such is the striking and delicate beauty of these dolomitic needles and the country about them that they deserve thorough and slow exploration. One road, through Vacqueyras, skirts the west side, and goes to Gigondas, the wine village. Nearly two kilometres nearer the Dentelles is the isolated Hôtel des Florets from whose terrace you can look from under the trees at the rocks on one side and the distant plain of the Rhône on the other. From this simple hotel one can walk, climb or ride.

Near Beaumes-de-Venise is a much admired example of rural Provençal architecture, the Romanesque chapel of Notre Dame d'Aubune, at the end of a grassy track off the metalled road. Sablet, Séguret, Crestet, Suzette and tiny, dainty La Roque-Alric all bask in enchanted corners of this unexpected piece of dramatic geology. Perhaps my favourite road is between Malaucène, Suzette and Lafare, with the golden evening sun pouring purple shadows from the Dentelles de Montmirail — the Roman *Mons mirabilis*, maybe — over the scented Spanish broom. Charles Martel is supposed to have defeated the Saracens in these hills in 739; hence Cimetière des Sarrasins, and Tour des Sarrasins near the hamlet of Montmirail. On such an evening it seems unlikely — and unimportant.

5 · THE LUBÉRON RANGE

Between Manosque and Cavaillon rise the Lubéron hills. The prospect of the southern flank, seen from the road which follows the Durance river, is unspectacular; villages are prosperous and the land yields well. The range is nearly 65 kilometres long and is cut by only one road from Cadenet to Apt, to divide it into Grand Lubéron to the east whose high point is 1,125 metres, and Petit Lubéron to the west. It is solid and inert, a slumbering boar. It does not advertise itself but merely waits discreetly. It is a great arched anticlinal fold separated from the sweeping Plateau de Vaucluse in the north by the wide valley of the Coulon which runs into the Durance below Cavaillon and carries the main road from Avignon to Upper Provence and the Alps. From the north the view is of abrupt slopes on which yesteryear's villages cling.

The Lubéron forms a compact world of its own in which to make unexpected discoveries. Forty years ago it was almost unknown. The few writers who commented on it found decaying châteaux, poor villages and inns that eighteenth century travellers might have recognised. Those writers almost gave the impression that theirs was the first white foot to tread these parts. Geographers of the ancient world who were familiar with other parts of Provence did not mention the Lubéron. Which is strange, for the N100 through Apt follows the Roman road, *Via Domitia*, pretty closely. In the Middle Ages the name *Lebredo* appears for the first time. Even the encyclopaedic Provençal poet, Frédéric Mistral, scarcely mentions it in his epic poem *Mireille*.

Today, comfort and tourism have reached it, yet it still succeeds in making the visitor feel something of a trespasser.

Cavaillon is the logical approach centre from the western side. This thriving, lorry-laden commercial dynamo for the fruit and vegetable industry of the region, has some interesting sights. In St. Véran it has a handsome church. Its synagogue is gay with wrought ironwork, and has a museum underneath which relates the history of the Jews in the Comtat Venaissin. There is a tiny Roman municipal arch, originally embedded in the wall of St. Véran, and moved stone by stone to where it is now in 1880. It is richly decorated but it lacks the military motifs of some other Roman arches, and was erected when Cavaillon was *Cabellio*. A stepped walk from near the arch leads up to Colline St. Jacques, 180 metres above plain and river, crowned by a rural chapel. The archaeological museum of Cavaillon contains objects found during quarrying work at the *oppidum* of the Cavares tribe on Colline St. Jacques — cooking utensils, things used by the tribe during its burial rites, Roman and Gallic coins.

Cavaillon offers three ways into the Lubéron. First, the northern road towards Apt, whose side-turnings reach a number of worthwhile villages. There is Oppède-le-Vieux, arguably the most impressive of the Lubéron villages. Its medieval and Renaissance houses had fallen into decay, but they are gradually being restored and lived in. On the hilltop are the solid church, partly Romanesque, partly 16th century, and the ruins of the 13th century castle built by Raymond VI, Count of Toulouse. It was he who handed it over to the Pope for the village to become papal property.

Or, a short distance away, Ménerbes, also with its back in the Lubéron and its views northwards across the plain of Apt towards the Plateau de Vaucluse. Here, too, restoration is taking place, and the 16th century château, a ramble of irregular walls, roofs, windows and turrets, has the simple charm of an old farmhouse.

Further east again is Lacoste whose massive castle is being slowly renovated by its present owner. Once it was one of the numerous Provençal properties of the notorious Marquis de Sade, the 18th century nobleman who gave his name to the word sadism, on account of his sexual practices and writings.

A second way into the Lubéron is by the Route de Crête du Lubéron. You take the Aix road (N573) out of Cavaillon and turn left after two kilometres. The narrow, twisting road rises steeply to follow the crest of Hautes Plaines and Massif des Cèdres to join the Cadenet to Bonnieux road. This is a scenic run of about 27 kilometres by the *route forestière*.

The third way is to continue along the N573 in the Durance valley. One of the sights along this road is the Gorges de Régalon, reached — in dry weather only — by a rough track along the bed of a torrent

The river Durance, the artery of Provence

between enclosing rock walls. Next, the road rises suddenly to the top of an escarpment and you are in Lauris. Just off the main road is a small, unassuming hotel, La Chaumière, half built into the top of the natural rock bastion of the village, high over the wide Durance valley. The view from the dining room is striking. Downstream is a distant sight of the sharp outlines of the Alpilles. Far across the opposite bank the village of La Roque-d'Anthéron is backed by the Chaine des Côtes. Upstream, the eye follows the lazy, silver serpents of water that slide between gravelly islets. Below, on flat ground, are gardens and reservoirs of water — the *bassins* of Provence — from which, in spring and early summer, rise the sonorous and indolent belchings of the frogs. "When the weather is bad elsewhere it is sunny in the Durance valley", remarked an earlier owner of La Chaumière. A little commercial patriotism, maybe, but I have usually known this valley in sunshine. True, to enjoy the views, you do not have to be in the hotel, but it provides the added pleasure of a good dinner served on attractive plate. To sit in the window and watch the valley's majestic sweep brought to incandescence by the setting sun is an invariably happy recollection.

Years ago the Durance was a scourge. In spring its swollen waters brought down the sharp smell of mountain air and the bodies of dead sheep, flooding low-lying land before rushing incontinently into the Rhône. Now, dams and canals, ramified over Lower Provence, have pacified the river. Its dramatic, even cleansing, role is over. It is an involuntary blood-donor to agriculture. Nonetheless, it remains for me the artery of Provence. Not the Rhône, an aloof international highway in transit until it reaches the Camargue, a frontier river between Provence and Languedoc. The Durance is part of the history and life of this country.

Beyond Lauris is Cadenet at the foot of a sand-yellow hill dotted with pines and cypresses, a ready-made background to an Italian painting of the Virgin and Child. It is pitted with caves, used as dwelling-places since prehistoric times. The church has a handsome bell-tower, and contains one of those curiosities often to be met with in Provençal churches where Christianity has adapted a pagan object. Here, the baptismal fonts were originally Gallo-Roman sarcophagi; on one can be seen the Gallic horned god Cernunnos surrounded by Roman deities.

Close to the level-crossing of the fruit and vegetable railway line for Cauaillon is the Hôtel Les Ombrelles, in its own garden. It has a large and cheerful restaurant and a few bedrooms in a single-storey annexe, another base from which to wander about the Lubéron.

On the other side of the river is the old Abbey of Silvacane (the Grove of Reeds), one of three Cistercian abbeys in Provence (Sénanque and Le Thoronet are the others). Founded in 1144 by hermits who ran a ferry service for travellers, it fell into decay in the 15th century, and restoration only began in 1949. Perhaps Silvacane is the simplest and loveliest of the three austere 'sisters', but all were built on low ground in expression of the Cistercian principle of humility.

As the main road beyond Cadenet moves away from the Lubéron range, lesser roads northwards can be taken to see some of the villages. La Tour d'Aigues has the extraordinary ruins of a once enormous 16th century château burned down in 1780. What is left intact is a monumental classical portal, like a 16th century reproduction of a Roman triumphal arch. Medieval Grambois, and the fortified walls and gateways of La Bastide-des-Jourdans, all these villages lying on the banks of the Lèze. Absurdly named Cucuron, with its massive houses, worn carvings, campanile and public wash-house.

Vaugines, Cabrières-d'Aigues, La Motte-d'Aigues. The names indicate the proximity to water, though most of the streams run from the Lubéron underground to bathe the stone roots of the old farmsteads. Ansouis is well-known because of the château of the Counts of Sabran whose descendants still live in it. The huge 17th century buildings are surrounded by fragments of a much older fortress dating back to the 10th century. Both the château and its gardens are open to the public.

Many of these names are associated with the 16th century inquisition in Provence directed against the heretical followers of Pierre Valdo, the 12th century merchant from Lyon who preached the Manichean views which rejected much of Catholic orthodoxy. They had been persecuted elsewhere and settled in the Lubéron where they were welcomed for their hard work and willingness to resettle declining villages. François I decreed that the Parliament of Aix should extirpate them. The Lubéron villages were destroyed. Most were

Sénanque (Vaucluse), one of three Cistercian abbeys

rebuilt but two, Tresemines and Cabrieretes were not, and orders were given for their names to be expunged from contemporary maps.

Lourmarin lies near the entrance to the white limestone combe which allows the only road-crossing of the Lubéron. It has grown a little in recent years, and even has a bypass, though it would be a pity to use it. Lourmarin embodies all the luminous gravity of the Lubéron. A specialised fame has come to it through its Renaissance château which, restored in 1920, was bequeathed to the Academy of Aix, and now provides facilities for artists and writers to work there. The major post-war novelist, Albert Camus, killed in a car crash in 1960, who had wished to put down his roots in Lourmarin, is buried in the cemetery. Lourmarin was also for long the home of Henri Bosco whose lyrical novels and elegaic poems about Provence and the Lubéron in particular give a fresh vision of an interior landscape. *"This blue Lubéron bathed in latin light"*, he wrote.

Partly because of my admiration for Bosco's works I remember with affection the Hôtel Ollier in the middle of the village. It stands there, thick-walled and massively arched. Red tiled floors and stairs, beamed rooms and Provençal furniture. It is many years since my wife and I stayed there when two old ladies endeavoured to run the establishment. It was at the Hôtel Ollier, before 1914, that Mistral, Léon Daudet and other friends feasted and recited poetry in Provençal, and Henri Bosco as a young man declaimed in his rich voice. The restaurant, I recall, had faded photographs of those distant days of Provençal literary revivalism. The Hôtel Ollier — unlike Le Paradou north of the village — does not make the guide books, but it has its niche in literary history.

Six kilometres up through the Combe de Lourmarin and the rough *maquis* country bathed in heat on either side, the road divides. To the right, it leads to the clean and lovely tower of St. Symphorien, all that remains of a priory, surrounded by the quiet of evergreen oaks. You can go on through Buoux along the D113, coming to crossroads at the ridge where the road descends to Apt, usually a marvellously deserted way.

Or the left fork takes you to Bonnieux. Charming corners, stepped streets, a fountain of two carved dolphins, a 12th century Provençal church surrounded by cedars at the highest point of the village, a newer church, three tiers or ramparts to hold Bonnieux to its crag, and distant views across the plain to the north. What more can one ask?

Approaching the Lubéron from Manosque or Forcalquier along the N100, the road from the east follows the Encrême stream to Céreste. Perhaps this had been Roman *Catuica*. There are some Roman foundations to the walled town set in fertile country. In the vicinity are various signs of the Roman presence. You are on the *Via Domitia*, one of the earliest highways from the Alps to Nîmes, Languedoc and Spain, and constructed under C. Domitius Ahenobarbus.

There is a Roman bridge over the Encrême outside Céreste. Not far away is a farm called Tavernoules where in Roman times, no doubt, there stood an inn, a *taberna*. To the west is the hamlet of La Bégude. Wherever you come across this name in Provence you know you are on a Roman road, for it is an old Provençal word for 'a place to drink', what the Romans called a *mutatio*. Apt, once *Hath* and capital of the Celto-Ligurian Vulgientes, became *Apta Julia* under Julius Caesar, though there are few visible remains.

Eight kilometres beyond Apt is the most perfectly preserved Roman bridge in France, the Pont Julien over the Coulon. Built in the 1st century A.D. it is still used. Powerful rather than elegant, it has a large central arch and a smaller one on each side. The massive blocks were laid without cement. At the foot of the arches are holes out of which, say the experts, looters of antiquity tore the strengthening bronze crampons. The arched apertures higher up in the masonry gave the waters of the Coulon when in flood an additional passageway through the bridge and so relieved pressure on the main arches. By the side of the bridge is a track parallel to the river (sometimes littered with rubbish and, in summer, smelly). This, I think, is the exact trace of the *Via Domitia*.

Ironically, one thing on the map that sounds cast-iron Roman but is not, is the Tour d'Embarbe, at the end of a lane off the Céreste-Apt road. This means the Tower of Ahenobarbus, the Domitius who built the *Via Domitia*, but the tower is a 12th century watch tower, and its name is an example of Provençal myth-making which likes to associate anything old with ancient Rome.

Apt has little of historic interest outside the church of Ste. Anne. Apt had been one of the earliest organised centres of Christianity in Gaul; the first church was put up in the 5th century over the remains of a Roman temple where Ste. Anne now stands. Three centuries later another church was erected. Charlemagne himself came on Easter Day 776 to consecrate it, and a carolingian altar is still visible in the upper crypt (there are two, superimposed), standing on a Gallo-Roman *cipous* or monumental pillar.

South of the N100 more delightful villages away from the main road repay a short visit — Castellet, Auribeau, Saignon whose church of various periods is especially delightful. North of the N100 are the ochre mines near Rustrel, Gargas and Roussillon. The iron-oxide workings reveal an astounding blood-red colour, even more intense than the *terra rossa* in the Arc valley near Aix. Walls, buildings and pathways are impregnated with it, and where workings have been discontinued, as at Rustrel, mounds of red clay stand out like so many gigantic tropical termites' nests.

Fifteen kilometres west of Apt, still on the N100, is Notre Dame-des-Lumières whose chapel is a place of pilgrimage; here the D60

Gordes (Vaucluse), slowly restored by artists

turns northwards towards Gordes. A little detour takes you through St. Pantaléon with an unusual Carolingian church; the foundations of the apse rise out of rock hollowed into what seem to be a number of tiny sarcophagi.

Gordes stands high on an escarpment of the Monts de Vaucluse, and the view carries the eye across the plain to Roussillon on its red cliffs. The plain looks prosperous; in imagination I can sympathise with the upland Provençaux who, with a tinge of jealousy, feel contempt for the fat living below. Gordes was one of the first villages whose ruins were slowly rebuilt by a colony of artists. It has a large church and a large Renaissance fortress-château, rather like Lourmarin's. Interesting rather than beautiful, as is the museum within — a display of Vasarely's kinetic art.

Scattered around Gordes, as well as at Bonnieux and further afield at Forcalquier, are the drystone buildings or *bories* which I mentioned in the historical survey of Chapter II. More than 3,000 of them have been mapped, some singly, others in clusters, on flat, stony ground where the materials are immediately to hand and require no trimming. They match their environment to perfection and illustrate the often enunciated principle that a building made of local stone cannot be ugly. Those *bories* in near-perfect condition are not more than 200 years old. Some are being restored for touristic use. The earliest are Neolithic. When these can be located they are merely a ring of scattered stones. They all use the architectural principle discovered by Neolithic man — the corbelled roof. In spite of the superior building technology introduced by Greeks and Romans into Provence, these *bories* continued to be built. The tradition is widespread, not only in other parts of France — and all bearing different local names — but also in Italy, Sardinia, Corsica, Spain, Portugal. They are the beehive houses of Scotland. Ireland and Wales know them. The shape varies, sometimes round or rectangular, single- or double-storeyed. They have been put to all kinds of use through the ages, not just as grain stores, as some have said. In the 16th century some were converted to blockhouses by the beleaguered Vaudois. When you see a cluster of these *bories* — and round Gordes they are visible from the roadside — surrounded by olive trees, you can picture them as the first tiny embryo villages created by the semi-nomadic pastoral peoples living with their flocks of sheep and goats off the sparse open country of little use to the settled agriculturalists who occupied the richer valleys.

6·THE VIRGILIAN ALPILLES

The Alpilles, separated from the Lubéron range by the Durance, are white, sharp and eroded. No point is higher than the 493 metres at l'Aupiho, though one could imagine the majestic ridge to be nearer the sky than that. It rises near Orgon and sinks at St. Gabriel near Tarascon on the Rhône. To the north and south the flatlands were a seabed in not-too-distant geological times, and the Alpilles were an island, and the Durance flowed into the sea through the narrows at Lamanon.

Why Virgilian? A classical poise and balance, perhaps, where proportions and values seem right; where one can believe man to labour willingly; where traditions linger in massive farmhouses among olive trees, pastures, shepherds' tracks, and the cypresses that fix the harmony of the landscape. This vision of an unbroken sequence of life is the accompaniment to any walk about the foothills, along the road between Maussane and Eygalières. Virgil has been the inspiration of every painter and writer of Provence.

St. Rémy-de-Provence is the tourist capital of the region, and the summer influx is intense. One of the less expensive hotels is the Des Arts, 30 Boulevard Victor Hugo, a central and cheerful base from which to explore. Maussane, ten kilometres away, is quieter and has two modestly priced hotels, Les Magnanarelles and L'Oustaloun. If you park the car under the plane trees in front of the latter you will spend an hour the next morning cleaning off the sparrows' droppings.

A short walk south from St. Rémy leads to the Plateau des Antiques. Set back from the road, on the right, surrounded by silencing turf and trees, stand two Roman monuments. On seeing them for the first time after a good lunch, Sir Winston Churchill turned to his companion, Lord Boothby, and said, "How bloody. How absolutely bloody." Let's have a sober look at each one.

Roman arch outside St. Rémy-de-Provence

Roman mausoleum outside St. Rémy-de-Provence

First, an arch, the oldest and smallest to survive in southern France. Erected around 20 B.C. at the entrance to the town of *Glanum* (on the other side of the road), its lightness betrays a Greek influence, and no arch in the south of France is more lovely. The reliefs commemorate the victories of Julius Caesar over the Gallo-Greek forces of Marseille in 49 B.C. with the by now familiar parade of captive Gauls, both men and women. On one panel, though, a Gaul is being granted his freedom. A mellowness of Roman outlook is also shown by the finely carved garlands of young fruits on the east face, while on the west face, the fruits have filled to autumn ripeness.

Rome, imperious and benign, fulfils its mission in the words of Virgil's *Aeneid*, "To spare the meek and battle down the proud".

Its neighbour is the almost perfectly preserved mausoleum which lacks only the pine-cone ornament of immortality on its cupola. Honey-brown and elegant, this cenotaph is twenty-five years younger than the monumental arch. It was put up in memory of Caius and Lucius, sons of Agrippa and adopted sons of Julius

The site of *Glanum* backed by the Alpilles

Caesar, who both died young. The Maison Carrée in Nîmes was dedicated to them, and other monuments to them were erected in Italy. Under the cupola are the statues of the brothers, while the carvings of Greek mythological scenes perhaps symbolise the lives of the two young princes.

An inscription on the north side states that this monument was erected by the three sons of one Caius, in memory of their parents.

Spelling and style prove that the inscription was added a century or more later. One wonders who could have had the nerve for such a piece of brazen status-upmanship.

In the Alpilles around the excavated site of *Glanum*, skeletons and primitive ornaments have come to light to indicate how migrants, traders and invaders of Neolithic and Ligurian times trod here. Some Gallic tribe settled by a spring deemed sacred during the 6th century B.C. Later came Phocaeans after the founding of Marseille. At first they traded with the Gauls, colonising the town 300 years later and calling it *Glanon*. The Romans arrived to find *Glanon* in ruins after the Cimbrian invasions of 102 B.C. Caesar occupied it in 49 B.C. and renamed it *Glanum*.

All these phases can be glimpsed in a stroll round the ruins, though the Hellenistic foundations are mostly overlaid by Roman ones. The buildings demanded by Romans for their comfort and as an expression of their civilisation are here. The baths, the gymnasium with hot, warm and cold rooms, a paved forum, two porticos, law courts and covered market united in a basilica, triumphal monuments, temples, shrines, statues, decorative carvings, mosaics (among the oldest in Gaul), houses and theatre which has been restored for present-day use.

Glanum flourished until 270 A.D. before its destruction by German tribes. The drainage channels constructed by the Romans became blocked and the site was covered with thick soil until excavations began in 1921. As yet, only about one tenth of a city which had a population of about 5,000 has been uncovered. Many of the objects have been removed to the archaeological museum in St. Rémy, so that it is more sensible to visit the site first and the museum afterwards.

Glanum stood on the Roman highway, the *Via Domitia*, on its way from Italy to Spain. The road passed under the arch. *Via Domitia* followed a much earlier track, sometimes referred to as *Via Heraclea*, the Road of Hercules. His name crops up in Provence from time to time, and one may well wonder why this Greek god appears here. A statue of Hercules was unearthed near the arch. A shrine to Hercules is exposed in *Glanum*. Numerous legends about the demi-god are associated with different parts of Provence. The god will have been imported from the eastern Mediterranean, but what he came to stand for was the telling of history through powerful story-images. He has acted as the liberator fighting against fearful odds, as the pioneer discovering new lands, as a healer — which is what he was at *Gla-*

num. Among his labours, he carried three golden apples from the Garden of the Hesperides along the *Via Heraclea* from Spain, through Languedoc and Provence into Italy. May this not be a storytelling about the bringing of a precious new metal, bronze? For bronze implements came by way of Iberia some 2,000 years B.C. with Cretan and other traders. Hercules also brought the cattle of Geryon by the same route. May this not be the telling of the new pastoral achievement of Neolithic man? Similarly, we can interpret the story of Hercules' fight against the Ligurians in La Crau, with the aid of stones hurled by Jupiter, as the bringing of a new social and religious order to this corner of Provence, as well as explaining supernaturally how all those stones came to lie on the flat wastes of La Crau. Monaco was dedicated to Hercules, as was explained in Chapter II, and Pliny said a port, identified as St. Gilles in the Camargue, was named *Heraclea* by the Dorians.

Vincent Van Gogh's asylum: cloister of Prieuré de St. Paul de Mausole

A short way back towards St. Rémy, on the same side of the road as *Glanum*, is the old Priory of St. Paul de Mausole. Along its entrance drive is a bust of Vincent Van Gogh who voluntarily confined himself here during an acute mental illness in 1889-90. In that period he painted some of his most luminous and expressive pictures which have transformed our vision of the south. From this asylum he continued to write letters to his brother Theo, just as luminous, just as expressive as his paintings. Van Gogh from the Netherlands where "the colours of the prism are veiled in mist", and Paul Cézanne from a few miles away in Aix; the one over-spontaneous, fevered to disintegration by Provence; the other dominating by will all impulses that deflected him from his clear artistic goals. Where else in the world have two such antithetical geniuses simultaneously illuminated the nature of things so profoundly?

Les Baux is crowded with sightseers, but it remains magnificent. The ruined buildings on the crest of the Alpilles are the colour and shape of the rocks, ground down molars in a jaw which juts out of the main line of the hills. Dante called them "battered tombstones"; it is thought that his *Inferno* was based on a visit to this place.

One guide book advises you to spend the night there to obtain the full thrill of it (the Hostellerie de la Reine Jeanne in the village is the most reasonable); another insists on a visit by full moon; a third counsels the sunset hour; yet another suggests a winter's day when the *mistral* is blowing. Most people who find themselves there on a hot summer's day will be in no danger of feeling isolated.

A well-preserved Celto-Ligurian camp shows that the site had been occupied long ago. The Romans were here, and two Gallo-Roman funerary monuments can be seen. In the 10th century the rock was seized by a feudal family which took the name *baou* (rock in Provençal), and later claimed descent from Balthazar, one of the Three Wise Kings. In medieval times the Courts of Love of Les Baux drew the most famous troubadours of the day; they honoured chivalry and courtesy, science and the things of the spirit. At its zenith 4,000 people lived there. In 1426 the princely house died out. In 1632 Louis XIII gave Les Baux to the Princes of Monaco who still bear the title. The eagles' wings of the Les Baux blazon have found their way into the heraldry of the House of Orange-Nassau of the Netherlands.

The streets are lined with more or less ruined medieval, Gothic and Renaissance buildings, many partly hewn out of the rock. The best-preserved Renaissance building is the Pavillon de la Reine Jeanne of

1581, except that it was not a queen but a baroness Jeanne of Les Baux. On a fine day you can see out across the Camargue to the sea, the best viewpoint being the statue to Charloun Rieu, a popular poet of Paradou, contemporary of Frédéric Mistral (and looking remarkably like him).

In the church of St. Vincent old and new meet — not everyone would say 'blend'. The oldest part of the building is from the 12th century. Some of the chapels are 17th century. The stained-glass windows were put in in 1960 as an offering by Prince Rainier of Monaco. One of the best known Midnight Masses of Provence is conducted here, and reflects the sustained attachment to the pastoral life. On Christmas Eve there is a procession of shepherds who make a ritual offering of a lamb drawn in a decorated cart. This ancient ceremony is very moving and is almost in the nature of a medieval mystery play. In the 16th century it was so filled with pagan profanities that the church tried unsuccessfully to suppress it. Other churches in Provence hold the *pastrage*, the Midnight Mass which identifies Christianity with the pastoral nature of the Nativity. You feel that, even now, this is totally appropriate to Provence.

Some make a sentimental journey to the Moulin de Daudet outside Fontvieille, which is a small Daudet museum. The celebrated *Lettres de mon moulin* — an almost obligatory phase of learning French — were not written here at all, nor did Daudet write them entirely himself; his collaborator was another Provençal fabulist, Paul Arène from Sisteron. The mill is a bit of a fraud.

What is genuine is an unusual relic of Roman industrial engineering which is not easy to find but worth the effort. From Paradou D78E is a minor road which wanders off towards Arles. Just before the Fontvieille crossroads you see the remains of two Roman aqueduct arches on each side of the road, remnants of a complex system of ducts from springs, one on the southern slope of the Alpilles, the other wending from the further side. You have to pick your way along an overgrown track to the left until you come in a few minutes to rising ground into whose incline was built, in the 4th century A.D the Barbegal water-mill. One of the aqueducts fed water through two parallel series of eight chutes to work sixteen hydraulic water-mills which ground local wheat for Arles, Rome and even further afield. The course of the mill-race and the slots for the grindstones are clearly visible.

Tarascon's castle took 150 years to complete. Its massive power dominates the Rhône. Less well known is a diminutive Alpilles, a low range of hills that is little more than an outcrop, wedged between the Rhône and the Avignon Tarascon road. This is La Montagnette which can be aerially surveyed from the top of Tarascon castle. Its eroded rocks are peppered with bushes and aromatic herbs, pines, cypresses, olives, vines, almonds and the ubiquitous broom. Here

Ruined Les Baux clings to the weathered Alpilles

Daudet's mythical *Tartarin of Tarascon* 'hunted his cap', a satire not just on the Tarasconnais but on all Frenchmen. Another corner of Virgilian Provence. The main town is Barbentane, a busy centre for the fruit and vegetable trade, its old part a jumble of narrow, cobbled streets, guarded by two medieval gateways and a 17th century château in white stone — a town which hardly knows about tourism.

Boulbon in the heart of La Montagnette is made picturesque by a ruined castle. On June 1st each year they hold the Procession of the Flasks or *Fioles* to the 12th century chapel of St. Marcellin. The story goes that Marcellin was a priest in Rome in 304 A.D. Refusing to sacrifice to false gods, he was hurled into a pit full of old jars. Just before he died he filled a jar with his blood and raised it in offering to the Lord. The blood was turned to wine, and St. Marcellin has become the patron saint of wine. Boulbon claims to have two reliquaries of St. Marcellin which are carried during the procession. The men bring bottles of wine to be blessed; the wine is then tasted as each man makes the Sign of the Cross. Afterwards, the wine is stored for use in the event of illness, especially fever. The sacred event is accompanied by noisy festivities of a thorough-going secular sort — as is any popular religious observance — for the origin of the Procession of the Flasks is, no doubt, Bacchanalian.

Close to Boulbon in the *garrigues*, or heathland, is another name made familiar by Alphonse Daudet, Abbaye St. Michel de Frigolet (*ferigoulo* is Provençal for thyme), the setting for the story of 'The Elixir of Father Gaucher'. This abbey was founded in the 12th century by the Benedictines of Montmajour, and is in use today.

Montmajour, about twenty kilometres south as the crow flies, is in ruins but being restored. Its monks spent centuries draining the marshes immediately below the rocky spur on which it stands, still an imposing and architecturally fine building, although something of a mixture of Romanesque church architecture and late medieval military architecture.

In danger of being overwhelmed by the abbey buildings is the 12th century funerary Chapel of Ste. Croix, all by itself a little way down the road. It is an exquisite little cruciform chapel with an apse on each side, a rectangular porch, and a graceful campanile perched aloft. It is surrounded by tombs dug out of the rock.

Between Graveson and St. Rémy, across intensively cultivated lands dissected by canals, lies the quiet village of Maillane, birth place of Frédéric Mistral, the poet whose fame spread far beyond the boundaries of Provence. He was born in 1830 in Mas du Juge. La

Maison du Lézard was where he lived for twenty-one years, while opposite is the Museon Mistral where he died in 1914. His statue stands in the garden. For many, Mistral is the supreme interpreter of Provence, who in poetry relived the greatness of the classical past. I am not sure if his greatness does not lie more in what he stood for than in what he wrote. He championed the revival of the Provençal language, in danger of being crushed by an over-centralised administration in Paris, when everything indigenous to Provence seemed to be 'Frenchified'. His passion for Provençal language, customs and traditions animated his encyclopaedic output, but his characters float motionless and weightless in formalised legend. They lack the full-blooded drama of the hero-myth; they lack the anguish of psychic conflict. They are a confection of a fictitious past.

7 · ARLES AND THE CAMARGUE

The rise to power of Arles in antiquity was linked to the commercial fortunes of the river Rhône, one of the few major rivers to run into the Mediterranean Sea. Arles sits astride the Rhône at the apex where the river divides into the Grand Rhône flowing southeast into the sea at Port St. Louis—an industrial offshoot of the port of Marseille and dealing with oil, liquid gas and chemicals, as well as wine, salt, cereals and wood—and the Petit Rhône which straggles southwest to gain the sea near Les Saintes-Maries-de-la-Mer. Within this triangle is the Plaine de la Camargue, technically an island. It is made up of rich silt brought down by the fast currents of the Rhône, so that much of the delta coastline encroaches on the sea.

Arles, the largest commune in France, is the central market for the agricultural produce of the region. It has the air of being the most Provençal of all the larger towns and, as Patrick Turnbull has neatly observed, Arles "is in sharp contrast with Avignon's pure feudalism, Aix's donnish reticence, and Marseille's aggressive modernity".

In remote times—certainly as far back as 1,000 B.C.—Phoenician traders sailed across the Ligurian Sea, *Ligusticum mare* of the old geographers, to trade along the coast and penetrate up the Rhône to exchange Greek produce for cereals, metals, amber. After the foundation of Marseille the Phocaeans set up a trading post at Arles, calling it *Theline*, or 'foster mother' which the Romans later translated into *Mamillaria*, in part to honour the immense fertility of the Camargue whose wheat harvests were as rich as those of the Nile delta.

By the 4th century B.C. *Theline* had been taken over by the Celto-Ligurian tribe of Saluvii who gave the place the Celtic name of *Arlath*, 'town near the swamps', later to become Roman *Arelate*. Much of the land south of Avignon was covered by shallow waters and shifting, pestilential marshlands. Such conditions made navigation hazardous and constantly threatened to strangle the livelihood of Arles as a lagoon port. The first systematic draining was undertaken by Caius Marius in 104 B.C., who dug a canal to link the Roman naval port at Fos with Arles, the *Fossae Marianae*. In the Middle Ages, the 'salt abbeys' of the Camargue (notably Ulmet, Sylveréal and Psalmody of which only tiny traces remain) continued the work of reclamation, and this has gone on ever since. Today, the land level of the delta is about ten metres higher than it was 2,000 years ago.

River and lagoon navigation was monopolised by powerful guilds of boatmen whose craft were frames resting on inflated bladders. The strongest monopoly of all was held by the *navicularii marini Arelatenses* who held exclusive rights to ferry wheat from Arles to Ostia, the port for Rome, and even further afield. Such became the power of these unions that when they raised a finger even the emperor had to pay heed.

In 49 B.C. Arles sided with Julius Caesar in his quarrel with Pompey. For Caesar's siege of Marseille, Arles provided him with a fleet of ships at a month's notice, and Arles' political prosperity under the Romans was assured. It became a colony for veterans of the Sixth Legion on the left bank of the Rhône; the natives were where Trinquetaille now is, and Arles came to be spoken of as *Arelate duplex*. Many trades flourished along with the naval dockyards. An engineer of Arles, Benignus, constructed the water-mill at Barbegal. As the Roman Empire declined, Arles' importance grew. It was known as the 'little Rome of the Gauls', and, after the foundation of Constantinople in 329 A.D., Arles became the second capital of the Empire. In 395 it was the political and administrative capital of Gaul, and the last bastion of Roman defence against invaders, finally falling to the Visigoths in 480.

The first Christian bishopric was established in 254 by St. Marcien, although a more fanciful tradition has it that St. Peter himself sent St. Trophimus to convert Arles in the 1st century. In 730 the Saracens occupied Arles, and between the 9th and 12th centuries it fell under various influences before its decisive absorption into the Kingdom of France in 1481. The terrible plague of 1720 decimated the population, but a measure of prosperity was retained through the commercial value of the Rhône. This lasted until the advent of the railway in 1845. More recently, in abandoning its role as port, Arles has profited from the new agricultural techniques applied in the drained flatlands round about.

Most of the old town is squashed between the lively, tree-lined

Arles, Museum of Christian Art: carvings on a 4th century sarcophagus

Boulevard des Lices (the lists, or tilting-ground) and the river, and sightseeing has to be done on foot. Since the major sightseeing in Arles is its Roman past, this aspect will be dealt with first: the amphitheatre, theatre, Alyscamps, the crypto-porticus and the Baths of Constantine, plus the transferred obelisk in Place de la République. There are some important museums. One of them, Musée Lapidaire Paien, contains one of the best collections in France of Gallo-Roman remains; in a second, Musée Lapidaire Chrétien, the collection of 4th and 5th century sarcophagi is second in importance only to the Lateran Museum in Rome.

It is not absolutely certain when the amphitheatre or arena was built, but there seems to be a conçensus of opinion which places its construction during the reign of Hadrian, emperor between 117 and 138 A.D. The colony had been founded in Caesar's time, and the Sixth Legion veterans would have demanded their blood sports as soon as they had settled, so it can be taken for granted that a wooden amphitheatre stood originally on the site which was swampy. Oak piles were used as foundations, and some of them have been found intact. The three towers protruding within the outer wall of the arena (which is larger than the one at Nîmes, but not nearly as well preserved) are medieval, for it was fortified in the 13th century, and contained two chapels and 200 houses. Architecturally, the empty arena may be interesting but, as Van Gogh wrote, its colour, vitality and *raison d'être* can be gauged only when bull-fights fill the stands in which the privileged once had their reserved seats and the rest crowded the upper tiers.

Neaby lies the Roman theatre. In contrast to the powerful mass of stone of the amphitheatre, the theatre, built earlier during the reign of Augustus, perhaps between 27 and 25 B.C., betrays a Greek delicacy common to the Roman theatres in Provence. The theatre was probably the first of the three public buildings—the amphitheatre and the circus are the other two—to be erected because it was here that the élite gathered for their entertainment. Their demands were satisfied first. Although it is in poor condition, it is interesting to see that, untypically, it was erected on flat ground which meant that masonry had to support the semi-circular *cavea* or auditorium. The building must have been sumptuously decorated, and some of the fragments are displayed in it. Heads of bulls—the insignia of the Sixth Legion—adorn the facade. In 1651 the famous 'Venus of Arles' statue, now in the Louvre, was found in it, as was the statue of Augustus in the Musée Lapidaire Païen. The tiers of seats have been only partially restored, while two slender Corinthian columns survive, known locally as 'the two widows', and probably used as a gibbet in the Middle Ages.

At the end of the Avenue des Alyscamps are the Alyscamps, for centuries one of the most prestigious burial places in Europe, even before the Romans colonised Arles. Dante mentions it in his *Inferno*. From the 4th century on its fame spread throughout Christendom, only to fall into decline in the 12th century when it was announced that the mortal remains of St. Trophimus had been removed from the Alyscamps to the cathedral. In Roman times, the *Via Aurelia*, highway from Rome, passed through this necropolis. And now, some surviving sarcophagi have been lined up by a cramped pathway, at the end of which is the partly ruined church of St. Honorat, originally dedicated to St. Genest, beheaded in the 3rd century. Happily, some finely carved sarcophagi are in the Museum of Christian Art. As to the meaning of the word Alyscamps, most people say it comes from *Elysii Campi*, the Elysian Fields. Other philologists come up with other views—Fields of Alyssum, our Sweet Alison, they say.

Nearer the river are the Baths of Constantine, known as Palais de la Trouille. They formed part of the imperial palace built by Constantine the Great—for Arles was his favourite city—and it was here that he held the Council of Arles in 314, the first official assembly of Christians in Gaul. Water for the baths was brought by aqueduct from Egyalières, Roman *Aqualeria*, 25 kilometres away in the Alpilles.

Traces of a Roman circus used for chariot races have been revealed at Trinquetaille. A 15-metre high obelisk of Egyptian granite, which stood at the end of the *spina*—the low wall down the centre of the race-track—was re-erected in the Place de la République in 1676, with suitably royalist inscriptions, by Louis XIV. When the Revolution came a century later, Republican inscriptions were

Les Alyscamps at Arles

The west porch of St. Trophime at Arles

roughly superimposed. In 1829, the four bronze heads of lions were tactfully put up to cover both inscriptions.

Underground, and reached from the Musée Lapidaire Chrétien in Rue Balze, is the Roman crypto-porticus which originally surrounded the forum. These huge grain stores have been excavated for centuries; only recently has the work been completed. Begun around 40 B.C., and enlarged later, the construction is in the form of an enormous U, each arm of which is 106 metres long. Great care was taken over drainage and aeration. Mortar with charcoal powder was used to absorb humidity. The flooring was covered with pitch-pine, and the temperature inside the building remained constant and preserved the vast stores of cereals (milled at Barbegal) and oil with which Rome was supplied by the *navicularii marini Arelatenses*.

Enough of Roman Arles. Medieval art, surviving in the church of St. Trophime, is one of the splendours of Provence. The cool and dim interior draws the eyes into the high vaults of the nave and narrow aisles; there are paintings, carvings, sarcophagi and Aubusson tapestries, but it is the west porch, seen in the brilliant light of the square that is the most magnificent feature. Elaborate reliefs cover tympanum, lintel and jambs, all executed with wonderful freedom, drawing inspiration from the carving techniques of antiquity. In these 12th century carvings of the Almighty surrounded by symbols of the Evangelists, Apostles, angels, the Adoration of the Magi and Shepherds, of saints, the Elect and the Damned is compressed the minatory religious messages of the Middle Ages. These are the awful texts for illiterate pilgrims on the interminable route to the shrine of St. James of Compostela in Spain, visual texts they well knew how to read. Similarly impressive carvings met the pilgrims as they came to the porch of St. Gilles in the Camargue.

Roman models were also copied in the carvings of the lovely cloister of St. Trophime where the oldest sculptures of the 12th century— —they include St. Trophimus himself—are the finest works. Delicate carvings of saints and scenes from the Old and New Testaments abound, and graceful pilasters support the heavy-shadowed Romanesque arches that surround the bright patch of light in the centre of the cloister.

The Museon Arlaten should not be missed. To call it a regional museum of ethnography would be enough to put anyone off. It is, in fact, a wonderful panorama of the life of Provence in the past. It was founded by Frédéric Mistral in 1896 and improved with the money he received on winning the Nobel Prize in 1906 (actually, he did not win the prize outright but shared it with a now totally obscure Spanish writer). So many aspects of the past of the *pays d'Arles* and Camargue are depicted, either by means of life-like models, paintings, objects or documents, that plenty of time is needed to pass through the crowded rooms. One or two of them contain items from Mistral's life, and documents and paintings of the *Félibre* literary revival of which he had been the mainspring. The labels on the specimens of therapeutic and magical herbs are in Mistral's own hand. There are some reproductions of Van Gogh's works. In the two years of his stay in and near Arles, between 1888 and 1890 he painted 300 canvases. Both the Restaurant Carrel and his house on Place Lamartine were destroyed by Allied bombing in 1944. The Pont de Langlois over the canal between Arles and Port-de-Bouc which he made immortal in paint was destroyed in 1926 but an exact reproduction of it has been put up on the same spot. There is, of course, a Rue Van Gogh in Arles, but the imperishable associations with his name are in the Arlesian landscapes.

The Camargue is a paradox. Some see it as a flat, monotonous, tatty region, mosquito- and tourist-infested. It is exposed to wind and sun alike. Parched in summer and half drowned in winter, it is at its most melancholic when it rains, for the rain does not merely fall, it wells up from underground; sky and sea and land become indistinguishable.

Yet to the naturalist the Camargue is one of Europe's richest storehouses of birdlife, and its salt-impregnated lagoons and banks possess special plant and animal life. Its huge horizons are exhilarating and sunsets are spellbinding. Mirages can be as vivid as any in an Algerian *chott*. Melancholy is part of the substance of the Camargue and has inspired tragic literature among writers who do not normally write tragically. This is still something of an enclosed world, in spite of tourism and modern agricultural techniques and low-flying aircraft. Traditions of stock-raising are retained, and the language of the Camargue contains words that are not used elsewhere, for they describe things peculiar to the Camargue.

Travelling south from Arles or St. Gilles, one comes first to rice plantations and other agricultural areas; here the marshlands are fresh water. Further on, the lagoons or *étangs* become brackish. Near the sea-dunes the *étangs* are strongly salty. Each of the three areas supports a different kind of vegetation. At the heart of the Camargue is the great Etang de Vaccarès, a nature reserve to which only accredited naturalists have access, which is at the centre of the conflict between the sweet waters brought down by the Rhone and the salt left in the soil by the retreating sea. The salt-impregnated southern parts are the poorer soils where horse breeding and cattle raising are now concentrated.

Black bulls and white horses first established the romantic fame of the Camargue. Various theories are put forward to explain their origins, but what is certain is that the Romans will have made sure there was an adequate supply of both for the arenas. The Camargue bull is

Camargue *gardians* on white horses, perhaps first brought by Saracens

a lighter, faster animal than the Spanish bull; the former is used for the usually harmless *course à la cocarde* dear to every little Provençal bullring, and the latter is used for the occasional *mis-à-mort*. The Provençal bull generally retreats on the approach of a human out in the open; its aggression is generated by the enclosed arena. The white horse is short, tough and broad-hoofed, bred to slog through the mud.

Tourism has done some harm to the Camargue, but it has also

Thatched *gardian* huts in the Camargue

brought one benefit. The cowboy vogue has halted the decline in breeding cattle and horses. The cattle no longer go for sausage meat but are groomed for the rings; the horses no longer die of neglect, disease and starvation as they did in the last century, for now the cowboy-for-the-day wants to ride them.

Even for the non-ornithologist, the birds of the Camargue are a delight. During a May visit, for instance, one might see stilts, pratincoles, little egrets and herons, bee-eaters—the most richly coloured birds of all—hoopoes, golden orioles, nightingales; about 300 species have been recorded. Then that most miraculous of all ornithological sights, a colony of flamingoes, perhaps glimpsed between Fiélouse and Salon-de-Badon, near the edge of Etang de Fournalet, or else the Etang de Galabert. A third viewpoint is near Mas de Cacharel where the birds can be seen in Etang de Malagroy and Etang dit l'Imperial. For these birds breed in the Camargue, irregularly and with difficulty, the only place in Europe where they do so.

Grotesque, misshapen and slightly ridiculous when feeding or performing domestic or social chores at the nest, when they take flight the pulse quickens at the sight and sound of a rising curtain of pink and white and black *flamants roses* or *flamencs* to the Provençal.

Les Saintes-Maries-de-la-Mer (it is much easier to call it by its Provençal name, *li Santo*) is an undistinguished little town by the sea, yet made striking by its church. Of all Provençal fortress-churches this one states its military-defensive function most clearly and austerely. It is an arrow-slitted rampart guarding an isolated fishing village against perpetual sea-borne threats. Four bells are slung aloft to call for help across desolate medieval marshes.

Originally, a temple of Mithras stood here on the spot which had been known as *Oppidum Ra*, 'the raised table-land'. A Christian oratory was superposed. It became too small to hold the pilgrims who came to worship where the miraculous boatload of saints who were to evangelise Provence had landed. It had to be enlarged in the 9th century, and the present church was built in the 12th century. The belief that the saints' remains were buried in the crypt seemed to be confirmed when in 1448 King René claimed he had found the bones

Fortress church of Les Saintes Maries-de-la-Mer

of St. Mary, sister of the Virgin, and St. Mary, mother of the Apostles John and James, and their servant Sara. The remains of the two Marys are enshrined in the upper church; those of 'black' Sara, the dark-skinned Egyptian, not having the right to canonisation, lie in the crypt.

On 24th and 25th May each year the painted images of the two Marys are carried in procession to the sea at *li Santo*, where they are blessed. At the same time, the gypsies worship the black-painted plaster image of Sara in the crypt, later carrying her for ritual immersion in the sea. By this act both the Church and the gypsies have adapted an ancient fecundity ritual, and healed the long-standing animosity between the Provençaux and the gypsies—the age-old conflict

between the settled farmer and the nomad. The gypsies referred to the peasants as *gadjé* or 'serfs'; the peasants called the gypsies 'Saracens'. A local legend says that Sara was the daughter of the priest-king of the bulls of the Camargue; she had a vision of the arrival of the saints in their frail bark, helped them ashore, was baptised and preached the Gospel among the *gadjé*.

Festivities continue for another day or two before the crowds disperse. The only other thing of interest in *li Santo* is the little Musée Baroncelli, with a collection of plants and animals of the Camargue. The Marquis Folco de Baroncelli-Javon (1869-1943) was the great poet-rancher who embodied all the qualities of the aristocrat-democrat of Provence.

North of the village is the Municipal Zoo where many of the Camargue birds can be seen in captivity. To the northwest lies Aigues-Mortes. The road crosses the Petit Rhône where the hamlet of Sylveréal is a reminder that the Camargue was well wooded in Roman times, yielded plenty of game, and was 'the granary of the Roman army'. A reminder, too, that the Camargue owes its name—perhaps —to Aulus Annius Camars, a wealthy landowner who in 83 A.D. ensured undying popularity with the people of Arles by stipulating

Curtain walls of Aigues-Mortes

that competitive games were to be held annually on the day of his death, in Arles' arena.

The ramparts of Aigues-Mortes (Dead Waters) are magnificently preserved. The town was founded by St. Louis as a port from which to sail for the Seventh Crusade. He bought the site from the monks of Psalmody (meaning 'salt', not 'singing'), built the circular keep of the Tour de Constance, and dug a channel to the sea. The walls of rectangular Aigues-Mortes were put up by Philip the Bold in 1272—you can walk round them—but the port's importance was short lived, for the channels to the sea silted up. In the Middle Ages what is today the D46 road was the only way across the desolate marshes to Aigues-Mortes, and the sentinel tower which obliges motorists to skirt round it—the Tour Carbonnière—was put up while the walls of the port were being built.

The motorist can make a complete circuit of the Plaine de la Camargue by using the metalled roads that skirt the Etang de Vaccarès, plus the Digue de la Mer, a bumpy, sandy track which threads its way between the lagoons, with a sand-spit between it and the sea to the south. The track, some sixteen kilometres in length, may be used only in dry weather. Nowhere does one get a better impression of the untouched Camargue, a region able to exert a strong and mysterious spell over its devotees.

8 · INSPIRATION FOR ART: MONTAGNE SAINTE-VICTOIRE

The spirit of three mountains dominates Provence: Mont Ventoux, La Sainte-Baume and Montagne Sainte-Victoire. At each may be celebrated an aspect of human achievement. Mont Ventoux stands for the humanistic achievement of man through Petrarch, and has already been discussed. La Sainte-Baume, where Mary Magdalene is said to have spent thirty years of solitary contemplation after her landings with the other saints at Les Saintes-Maries-de-la-Mer, represents the Christian achievement. Montagne Sainte-Victoire which Cézanne painted again and again, stands for creative achievement.

The twelve kilometres of buckled limestone which is Ste. Victoire surges out of the plain of Aix east of Aix itself and sinks away between Puyloubier and Pourrières. Its highest point at Pic des Mouches is a little over 1,000 metres, though it is the tall iron cross at Croix de Provence that catches the eye. From whichever compass point I see that impressive mountain I find my spirits raised. At the midday hours of summer the abrupt southern flank is a white-hot furnace, heated—I can easily imagine—by flames, which are the brilliant red-brown soil, that lick its lower slopes, and the dark pine trees are the rich green smoke. At dawn, the pale lilac of its profile is scarcely distinguishable from the morning sky, and as the sun goes down majestic heavy-shadowed yellows and reds seem to well out of the rock.

Separating Ste. Victoire and the Massif de la Sainte-Baume to the south is the valley of the river Arc which carries the auto-route and the N7 that more or less follows the ancient Roman highway from Italy, the *Via Aurelia*. Near the village of Pourrières a momentous battle took place on April 24th—it is surmised—in 102 B.C., when the Roman general Caius Marius annihilated a great army of Teu-

Southern face of Montagne Sainte-Victoire

tons and Ambrons intent on invading Rome. It is sometimes said that Ste. Victoire was so named in honour of the famous victory, but in reality the origin is the same as Mont Ventoux's. Both had been sacred mountains in pre-Roman times when wind gods—Ventour or Vintur—had been worshipped. Later, the names were latinised as Vencturus. With the arrival of Christianity the mountain had a variety of names such as Sainte-Aventure, Sainte-Venture, Sainte-Bonaventure, before Sainte-Victoire was settled on. Even today, the people of the Arc valley are known as Venturi.

The only knowledge we have of the battle comes from Plutarch writing some two centuries after the event. He described the battle dramatically. Later writers, like Sir Walter Scott in *Anne of Geierstein*, embellished it. 100,000 enemies of Rome were killed that day; more—women as well as men—took their own lives; many more went into slavery. The little river Arc ran red with blood, and so choked with corpses was it that its course became altered. For years afterwards local farmers found bones and used them to mark the boundaries of their little vineyard plots. Barbarian blood, the story went, stained the soil to the deep red of the *terra rossa* it is today. It fitted the whole story neatly to say, as philologists have said, that Pourriéres derives from *Campi putridi* on account of the putrefying bodies. It could more likely mean a field of leeks. But the great fire which Marius commanded, according to Plutarch, at the tile factory of *Tegulata* (now La Petite Pégière or Pugère), may well have been pinpointed when the debris of a holocaust was revealed in the last century. And on the hill of Pain de Munition nearby is a still visible Roman fortification—*Annonae munitio*—which formed part of Marius's contingency plans should the battle go adversely.

South from Pourrières towards the N7 I have often passed a jumble of stones almost invisible in long grass, fondly thinking they were the last remains of a triumphal arch Marius had built to commemorate the victory. On the pyramid was a bas-relief of Marius standing on his shield and hoisted aloft by his soldiers. So the experts had said. But the archaeologist, Fernand Benoit, says the monument had been a mausoleum and had no connection with the folk-hero Marius. It is also a myth that so many Marseillais are given the name Marius in honour of the general. Until Napoleon came along grandiosely infatuated with Roman antiquities and heroes nobody was baptised Marius. In any case, Marius is a convenient masculination of the Mother of Christ whom the Catholic Marseillais venerate.

Today, our view of Ste. Victoire is inescapably coloured by Paul Cézanne who was born and died in its shadow. He tells us about the reality of the Provençal landscape for he, unlike Van Gogh, was a native who embodied the Mediterranean passion for balance, harmony, rationality, clarity. He wanted to convey the eternity of nature. Critics can find much fault in his work. Lesser artists have been better draughtsmen; lesser landscapists have depicted the mineral textures better; Cézanne lacked inventiveness; he obsessively repeated certain themes over and over; his view of nature was naïve; he treated landscapes as though they were still-lives and he excluded the human form from them; his portraits are expressionless—again, still-lives. Yet he came to be seen as the greatest revolutionary in art since Giotto, and he has stamped his influence on almost all artists to have followed him.

Cézanne wanted to depict nature as eternal; it was an artistic passion held with religious devotion, and Ste. Victoire was his high altar. Obsessively he willed order out of chaos, certainty out of hesitation. His veneration of Ste. Victoire is conveyed by the upward exaggeration of its proportions in his paintings. Eternal nature may seem an archaic view to modern man whose dominion over nature is asserted with ruthless uncertainty. An archaic view, perhaps, but one that will endure in the history of art.

After Cézanne had worked through his romantic and erotic

phases in painting he evolved an unromantic attitude towards the Aixois countryside he seldom left and which was the source of his creative energy. Rather, one senses a latent hostility, a tension between him and his *motif*, as though the scene got in the way of his striving for greater clarity and truth.

These aspirations become more understandable as one knows a little more about the man himself, though it is a paradox that he himself detested self-revelation. He was often taciturn and solitary. His political attitudes were reactionary, his public ambitions almost pathetically *petit bourgeois*. He would emphasise his sense of inferiority by repeating, "*Moi, qui suis faible dans la vie*", "me, so weak in life". This was the mask of the strong willed creator who presents his external self as weak and in need of support.

Paul Cézanne was born at Aix-en-Provence in 1839, five years before his parents married. His father was a hatter who bought the only local bank and made a fortune. The boyhood friendship between Cézanne, Emile Zola and Baptistin Baille was a relationship of great intensity, of the sensory experience of the countryside, of pranks, rambles and daydreams. In 1858 Zola went to Paris, and Cézanne was left feeling aimless, touchy and unsure. His father sent him to the law school in Aix where he began an interest in painting. Three years later his father allowed Paul to join Zola in Paris but it was an unhappy and confusing place for him. Much of his work was wild, with a curiously unnatural freedom of brush-strokes, unsteady, an imitative romanticism. Later his canvases became grandiose and erotic, fantastical expressions of unreleased biological needs. Violent, timid, assertive and full of humility by turns—a duality reflecting the conflict between the corporeal and the ideological, between release and restraint, creation and guilt. These characteristics he never lost, only learned to harness.

Back in Aix in 1869 Cézanne met Hortense Fiquet when she was nineteen. A son was born in 1872, but the couple were not married until 1886 when Cézanne was no longer in love with her. Soon afterwards his father died, and the son inherited the fortune.

The year 1872 marked the beginning of Cézanne's control of his wayward temperament. He came under the benign and gentle influence of Camille Pissarro and, thirty years later, when at last a Cézanne was hung in the Paris *Salon*, he put *'élève de M. Pissarro'* after his own name in the catalogue.

The friendship between Cézanne and Zola was severed with the publication of Zola's novel *l'Oeuvre* in 1886, for the failed artist in it depicted Cézanne. Their mutual affection remained a mere undercurrent, yet the break was a necessity. Zola's vain and wordly influence had held back the development of Cézanne's artistic integrity. Loneliness was part of the renunciation of everything that interfered with the realisation of his sensations, as he put it. So completely did he live out his life in art that there was little human contact. He had a phobia about being touched; he could not work with female models. He developed a sense of persecution; he was mean in spite of his wealth; he destroyed much of his own work. By self-inflicted monasticism could he reach the truth of nature and work towards perfection.

His health deteriorated—he had diabetes—but he painted *sur le motif* to the last, to die in October 1906 after catching a chill while out painting.

It took a long time for recognition of his genius to come about. The Aixois did not approve of Paul Cézanne; he disliked them. The city of his birth was slow to appreciate him and when it did, it was too late; it could not afford to buy his works for the Musée des Beaux-Arts. But now, of course, everyone pays him tribute. There are innumerable associations with his life: his birthplace in Rue de l'Opéra; his school; the Jas de Bouffan, the family seat; the road past Le Tholonet where the dusty café of his day still stands; Château Noir and the quarry of Bibémus where he painted; his handsome studio in Chemin des Lauves as it was then, and now (of course) Avenue Paul-Cézanne; all the places he and Zola and Baille visited in their youth. There are many points at which the pilgrim will wish to stop, but the chief monument to Cézanne is the Aixois countryside.

Self-portraits have made Paul Cézanne's appearance familiar. To give greater depth, here is a revealing passage by Edmond Jaloux, a Marseillais writer who met Cézanne at the end of the 19th century, and left this portrait in *Fumées dans la campagne* (my translation). "Suddenly the door opened. Someone came in with an almost exaggeratedly cautious air. He gave the appearance of being lower middle-class or else a comfortably-off farmer, artful and formal at the same time. He was a bit round-shouldered; white hair escaped in locks; his small eyes were piercing and prying, a rather red Bourbon nose, short, drooping moustaches, and a military goatee beard. That was how I saw Paul Cézanne at our first meeting, and that is how I always see him.

"I can hear his way of speaking, nasal, slow, meticulous, with something solicitous and caressing in it. I can hear him discoursing on art or on nature, with subtlety, dignity and profundity.

Aix-en-Provence, birthplace of Cézanne: Fontaine des Quatre Dauphins

"One day when he was having lunch at our house, he looked at some apricots and peaches lying on a platter, and he said to us:

" 'See how tenderly the light loves the apricots; it possesses them wholly, it enters their flesh and it lights them up all over! But it is miserly towards the peaches, for it illuminates no more than half of each fruit.'

"In this way he made wise little remarks which nobody seemed to have made before. On another occasion, he said to Cordouan, as I strolled along the Rue Cardinale with them:

" 'An artist, you see, ought to do his work as an almond tree makes its flowers, as a snail makes its slime....'

"When he had left the Pavillon de Suffren, Maurice got up solemnly and said to me:

" 'Raymond, remember this man's words. Later on you will be proud to have been near him and you will be able to boast, "I knew him too!" ' "

In Aix-en-Provence the Musée des Beaux-Arts (more popularly known as Musée Granet after the 19th century painter who, with others, gave the original art collection to the town) is a first-class provincial art gallery. In it, Cézanne can be placed in context; there are works by his Provençal predecessors and successors. Those who came before him were little masters of naturalistic achievement, expressing their love of Provence by painting what they saw, their fame overshadowed by the master of Aix. Yet they are a delight to anyone who wants to relate art to landscape and note the historical development of landscape out of Christian constraint and classical formalism to an art form in its own right.

First, it is worth looking at others who had painted Ste. Victoire. J.A. Constantin was perhaps the first artist in Europe, in 1780, to paint from nature out of doors—*sur le motif*—almost a century before Cézanne. His view of it hangs in the museum, along with numerous 19th century portraits of the 'magic mountain' by F.M. Granet, M. Engalière and Paul Guigou, the finest landscapist before Cézanne—see how he represents colour, clarity and texture; twelve of his works hang here. Ste. Victoire is also in paint at the hand of Félix Ziem and Adolphe Monticelli, an artist of vibrant and jewel-like effects who impressed Van Gogh.

There are many other Provençal landscapes, including moderns such as René Seyssaud, Yves Brayer and A. Chabaud, but the most eye-catching of all is Emile Loubon's huge *Les Menons de Crau*. This is a supple and dramatic portrayal of an advancing flock of

Cloister of cathedral of St. Sauveur, Aix-en-Provence

rams. Other works by Loubon are here, as well as two portraits of him painted in mid-19th century, but his most famous work is the large view over Marseille with cattle and drovers which is in the Beaux-Arts at Marseille.

On a wider perspective the Musée Granet has valuable collections of paintings from Italian Primitives through various European schools down to the present day, while its archaeological displays are of importance for the Celto-Ligurian sculptures retrieved from the *oppidum* at Entremont.

Aix is a town of sober charm, whether one strolls along Cours Mirabeau, arched over with great plane trees which in 1830 replaced the 17th century elms, and cooled by the sound of its fountains, or else round the stately mansions of the 17th and 18th centuries. The cathedral of St. Sauveur is a jumble of styles, a veritable museum with its 5th century baptistery, its seventeen Flemish tapestries of 1511, the 16th century door panels, and the great masterpiece—the

Burning Bush triptych by Nicolas Froment of Uzès, completed in 1476. The stylised countryside background is Provençal; the figures are Flemish; the grisaille work is Gothic. This richly painted work was commissioned by King René for his sepulture. Near the baptistery exit are the 12th century cloisters.

Of museums there is no shortage. The Pavillon de Vendôme, built in the 17th century, is a perfectly proportioned country house, furnished in the 17th and 18th century styles. Both the Musée de Vieil Aix and Musée Paul Arbaud have collections relating to the past of Provence; Bibliothèque Méjanes contains one of the richest collections of books and manuscripts in France. A little to the north of Aix is the Plateau d'Entremont where the remains of the religious and political capital of the Saluvii tribe can be visited. They occupied this site from the beginning of the 3rd century B.C. until the Romans destroyed it in 123 B.C. Some of the ramparts and towers are clearly visible, as are some ballista balls which bombarded the place into submission.

9 · FROM SISTERON TO THE SEA

Sisteron makes the most dramatic entry into Provence. Like half-opened curtains on a natural stage set, the limestone barrier of the southern Pre-Alps is parted here by the river Durance and its tributary, the Buëch. The town crouches on guard and looks southwards towards a wide, slow valley that divides the Plateau de Valensole on the east side of the Durance from the smaller Bassin de Forcalquier on the west. This is rich alluvial land compared with the gaunt, fleshless ribs of the Dauphiné hills which have just been left behind. In sheltered places the first olive trees appear, and life is gentler here. Rail and road communications are easier, and there is industry in the valley. A peasant economy which had clung to an enclosed fallow-system has given way to fertilisers and machinery, drought-resistant crops such as sainfoin and lavender which bring in cash. Lavender is still a source of wealth to Upper Provence, even if somewhat in decline now. Above 600 metres true lavender is grown for quality; below 600 metres the hybrid *lavandin* is grown for quantity.

Sisteron is built on the west bank of the Durance, at the foot of a huge rock whose heavily folded strata stand out like the straining muscles of an Atlas; they bear the weight of the citadel that commands the defile and the suburb of La Baume on the opposite bank, reached by a single-span bridge. In spite of a destructive aerial bombardment in 1944 when the Germans were already in full retreat, one can still wander through a warren of narrow, stepped and arched streets called *andrônes*, and tiny squares. Notre Dame, once a cathedral, is a finely proportioned church of the 12th century.

The main street burrows under the citadel by means of a tunnel, and passes the church. It is Avenue Paul Arène, in recognition of the writer of Sisteron who, in 1866, collaborated with Alphonse Daudet in writing the celebrated *Lettres de mon moulin* under the pseudonym 'Marie-Gaston'. These letters were written in Paris for Parisians who came to think of Provence as the quaint and distant place the 'Letters' made it out to be. Later, the two men fell out and Daudet acquired all the honours for the book. Both were fine literary craftsmen in a delicately miniature way. Arène's best-known book, *Jean-des-Figues* (1868) is an insubstantial semi-autobiography, of lively, mannered descriptions of his native Sisteron, slightly masked under the name 'Canteperdrix'. His conversation, like his books, was bright, quick and polished. Anatole France found him a reserved Southerner whose facial muscles never moved when he spoke.

Most motorists take the N85 south from Sisteron, the *Route Napoléon*. There is a lesser, left-bank road, from which the rear of Montagne de Lure's hump can be seen rising out of the valley. This road goes through Volonne, stuck against a rocky spur supporting

Citadel of Sisteron, gateway into Provence

two towers of a medieval castle; what is now the Touring Hôtel is the house where Napoleon spent the night of March 5th 1815 on his return from Elba. Across the river is Château-Arnoux and industrial St. Auban, of interest to the traveller merely in the reflection that its electro-chemical works process chlorine derivatives from salt produced in the Camargue, as well as bauxite mined in the Var; finished aluminium is despatched northwards.

A nicer route is to leave N85 six kilometres out of Sisteron to follow the 700-metre contour round Lure to Forcalquier. It takes you by Mallefougasse and a château, and Cruis with a Romanesque church. At Cruis you can turn back on a rough track in the direction of Notre Dame de Lumière to find a broad, well-preserved section of Roman road, part of the great *Via Domitia* from Italy to Spain. Next is the little resort of St. Etienne-des-Orgues from where a road zigzags to the highpoint of Lure, the Signal de Lure at 1,826 metres. On the way up you come upon two oratories on the right of the road. A path leads down a ravine to Notre Dame de Lure surrounded by massive lime trees. This hermitage was founded by St. Donat who evangelised the region around 500, having travelled there by way of the *Via Domitia*. South from St. Etienne the narrow, winding D12 leads through Fontienne to Forcalquier.

A few fairly modest hotels serve the needs of business travellers and people coming to market more than tourists; the relative lack of tourists leaves Forcalquier with an invigorating air of unselfconsciousness. Yet it has plenty to offer, as does its countryside. Not far away, for the astronomer, lies the Observatoire National d'Astrophysique de Haute-Provence, just outside the village of St. Michel, which can be visited on certain days of the month. Or Mane's large Benedictine priory reached by a path from the main road (N100). Its massive and austere front is finely decorated with carvings about the portal, Corinthian pilasters, and a much-worn Christ in Majesty in the tympanum. Inside are frescoes and more carvings. Over the river Laye nearby is a Roman bridge. Also on the N100 is Château de Sauvan, an elegant 18th century building, handsomely furnished. Nearer the Durance and standing on a plateau 300 metres above it, is the Ganagobie Priory where restoration is still going on. First mentioned in 939 AD, the Priory suffered some destruction during the Revolution, but the carvings in the tympanum above the doorway have a simple, direct appeal. Yet the whole entrance looks odd. It has an oriental flavour. The two arches round the porch are finished off with scalloped or lobed stones, as is the door surround. In spite of being partly ruined inside, the building is full of interest for its 12th century mosaics and architectural originality.

A painting of the Virgin and Child by Adolphe Monticelli (1824-86) hangs on the left-hand wall of the nave. Near the chapterhouse is the cottage where Monticelli spent his poor boyhood. At the age of 25, after two years in Paris, he began his unending wanderings through Provence on foot, sometimes alone, sometimes with other painters, particularly Paul Guigou from near Apt, sometimes with Cézanne. This part of the Durance valley remained his solace and inspiration throughout his rather sad life. Between 1870 and 1883 he painted 2,500 canvases which he sold to passers-by in the Canèbiere in Marseille. He took to absinthe. The last phase was sordid, redeemed only by the presence of the woman he had always loved but who had refused to marry him, his cousin Emma Ricard; she cared for him until he died. Van Gogh called him a true painter, and aspired to be the continuation of Monticelli in Provence. If he is remembered mainly for his mannered genre paintings, his greatest works were still-life, landscapes and portraits; in these he achieved an intuitive vibrancy, purity and pathos. The painting at Ganagobie is not of his greatest, but it is a reminder of the originality of this artist, rooted in his Provençal homeland.

Back to Forcalquier. Its name in the Middle Ages was *Furnus calcarii* or limekilns. It stands on a cone, visible from a long way off. With a population of little over 3,000 it is large enough to generate a life of its own, and small enough for village intimacy. In the big central square are stalls of fruits and vegetables on market days. (I have still to discover exactly what the dried herbs are which the old man sold us as *bon pour les yeux*.) A side of the square is occupied by the one-time cathedral, a massive, impressive but rather gloomy and down-at-heel edifice which does not tempt me to go in, even though its rose window glows in the interior gloom. In front, an old fountain commemorates the marriage of Henry III of England to Eleanor of Provence in 1235, an event which led to a flood of foreigners occupying positions of importance in England, and the flouting of Magna Carta under this rather incompetent king. You can stroll round the old, narrow streets, the Jewish quarter and synagogue, look over the conventual buildings, or the little museum in the town hall, the Gothic fountain, the citadel's terrace where the surrounding hills are identified on a *table d'orientation*. The cemetery, outside the town to the northeast, is both enormous and neatly kept. Among the graves are those of Sir Jack Drummond, his wife and daughter, all murdered not far away at Lurs in 1952. In all likelihood this had been a tragic muddle in which Gaston Dominici thought he heard trespassers on his lands, and Sir Jack, camping for the night, thought the old man was a marauder; in the confrontation of two outraged men, Dominici let fly with his gun. But the trial never cleared the matter up properly. Also in the cemetery are some drystone pointed *cabanons*, related to the Neolithic *bories*, discussed in Chapter V.

South of Forcalquier is Manosque above the Durance. In spite of its peripheral clutter, something of the old town is guarded behind the encircling boulevards. Hôtel Terreau provides only bed and

Typical wrought-iron cupola: Notre Dame, Manosque

breakfast, but a bedroom facing the spacious Place Terreau where the car can be left, looks over plane trees to the 18th century wrought-iron belfry of St. Sauveur. In the church of Notre Dame is a Virgin and Child in black wood, perhaps the oldest in France.

The uplands north of Manosque are little known—simple, empty landscapes and wide, windswept prospects. They are the main characters in many of Jean Giono's novels. He lived most of his life (1895-1970) in a house on Mont d'Or outside Manosque, and is buried in the cemetery. A prolific writer, a master fabricator of myths of such persuasiveness that the wanderer in these parts becomes enmeshed in "his mythical domain, much closer to reality than are the history and geography books", as Henry Miller admiringly said. The settings for his stories are in Giono's upland Provence, but their meaning is universal, timeless and immediate.

A story is frequently repeated that the beautiful daughter of the consul of Manosque, in order not to be the subject of unwelcome attentions from François I on a visit to Manosque, disfigured her face by holding it over burning sulphur. This earned the town the name of Manosque-la-pudique, Manosque-the-chaste. I prefer the sobriquet Jean Giono gave it—Manosque-des-plateaux.

Downstream from Manosque the Durance is pushed into the narrows of the Défilé de Mirabeau, and from the other side of the river a rural road (D11) goes to Jouques. As the road drops towards the village in its wide basin a distant view of Montagne Ste. Victoire comes in sight. In the foreground is the deep yellow of the ripening wheat (in June, that is), and in the mid-distance is the low line of Montagne des Ubacs, the apotheosis of the big Provençal landscape. Jouques is the first of a string of villages along the eastward road which cuts through the centre of Provence. Rarely overburdened with traffic, it passes through open valleys, hills, woodlands, undramatic but satisfying scenery all the way to Draguignan and Grasse. Each village has its distinctive character and appearance.

Jouques, straight and with a wide main street and large plane trees, owns two cheerful fountains perpetually bubbling. One is outside the Auberge du Réal, a simple little hotel that looks out on what might pass, in a fit of absent-mindedness, as a village cricket ground. Searchers after archaeological trivia can make a base at Jouques. At La Traconnade, a little to the east, are the remains of Roman aqueducts which carried water to Roman Aix. There are more aqueduct arches nearer Meyrargues. A Bronze Age Ligurian *oppidum* whose outer walls are still discernible stands on Montagne de Lingouste to the east of Jouques, and a large Neolithic ruin can be traced near the Défilé de Mirabeau. Beyond La Traconnade, and a little to the right of the road, is the curiously named Chapelle St. Bacche, which leads to the natural supposition that once a temple for the worship of the wine god Bacchus was Christianised long ago on this spot.

The road towards Draguignan crosses one of the newer sections of the Canal de Provence whose waters flow by gravity from the Durance and Verdon rivers. The canal has already blended successfully with the landscape. Although the road skirts Rians, it is worth walking round the narrow arcaded streets and miniature square. Just before Esparron is the squat, heavily buttressed 12th century Chapelle du Revest surrounded by oaks; an earlier chapel had been destroyed by the Saracens. Then on the right is the solid hillside castle at St. Martin-de-Pallières.

Varages sits on a honeycombed tufa rock, and just south of it is a renovated chapel, nothing special to look at, but whose curious story illustrates the undercurrent of paganism in Provence. Chapelle St. Pothin was given this name by Protestants in the 17th century to efface the disgraceful name by which it had been previously known—St. Foutin. St. Foutin had been widely worshipped in Provence by men seeking potency and women fertility or else cures for shameful diseases. In the chapel stood a carved wooden object, shaped like a phallus and covered with leather. Wine was poured over it into a vessel, later to be used in secret rituals. The worshippers placed their ex-votos in the chapel; they were wax replicas of sexual parts. A chronicler was scandalised by all this, and by the fact that some men of Varages bore the surname Foutin, and even a girl had been named Foutine. The Protestants did away with all traces of this practice, even down to the name of St. Foutin, which has the same root as an obscene word for 'semen'.

The outside of the church of St. Maximin lacks towers and transepts; the huge facade above the west doorway is unfinished, but the choir is sumptuous. The 16th century painting by Francesco Rozen is of twenty-two panels of the Passion whose background includes the earliest known view of the Palace of the Popes at Avignon.

From Seillons minor roads go through Châteauvert and the narrow, tree-lined gorge of Vallon Sourn to Correns, thick-walled and enclosing twisted streets, to Montfort-sur-Argens, noteworthy for its subterranean chapel. Carcès, popular because its reservoir created in 1936, is good for fishing. A slight deviation from the Argens itself, through the vineyards, takes one to the impressive Cister-

Le Thoronet abbey, a restoration faithful to the original

cian abbey of Le Thoronet, set as these retreats always were in a lovely natural depression near water. Originally erected in the 12th century, it fell into disrepair when the monks were driven away by the Revolution. Restoration began in the last century on the orders of Prosper Mérimée, and today the red stone emerges severe and pure, an exact reproduction of the original abbey.

There is another diversion on the north bank of the river. On the secondary road between Lorgues and St. Antonin-du-Var is, to my mind, one of the most delightful of wayside chapels. Notre Dame de Ben Va, that is, Bon Voyage, is tucked a little way from today's road, and is reached by a lane scarcely wide enough to take a car. Very simple, partly built into the rock, an arch extends from the main body of the tiny chapel, across the lane which was once the highway. The real interest in the place lies in the murals which decorate this arch of a chapel erected in the 16th century at a time when the plague was ravaging the countryside. You can make out St. Fiacre, St. Maur and St. Blaise, and the Virgin carrying the Child who plays with a bird. By her side is St. Joseph leaning on his staff. There is also St. Christopher, the infant Jesus sitting on his shoulder and hanging on to his hair, while the saint plunges a tree trunk into a stream. The murals within the chapel which can only be peered at through a grill are in better state and there are more of them. It is a delightful site in which to spend a few reflective moments.

The Argens passes Vidauban, a wine town on N7, and on the *Via Aurelia* in Roman times; this part is still sometimes called *le pays aurélien*. There is a ruined Roman bridge near the place called Pont d'Argens, and it was at this *Pons argenteus* that Mark Antony encountered Marcus Aemilius Lepidus in 43 B.C.—they with Octavian formed the short-lived Triumvirate after the murder of Julius Caesar—to divide between them all the Roman dominions. Dissenting from these arrangements was Senator Laterensis who took his own life at this bridge.

Roquebrune-sur-Argens is picturesque and perched over the now widening valley of the river. There are both walks and drives in the vicinity, particularly to Montagne de Roquebrune, from whose summit are extensive views of the sea and the Alps. Fruit trees and vineyards utilise the alluvial soil of the open valley which separates the Estérel and Maures mountains. The main road runs into Fréjus which lies a little north of the mouth of the Argens. It is virtually fused with St. Raphaël, the Brighton of the Riviera, a cheerful, solid, year-round resort and very French. The long, sandy beach of Fréjus-Plage is split by the Argens from the straggling resort of St. Aygulf.

A similar priapic cult was practised in Embrun and Orange until its destruction by the Protestants, but pilgrimages to chapels where it was believed that women would be assured of fecundity were once common. Some chapels carry the symbolic name of Notre Dame des Oeufs. Observances of this nature did not die out until the beginning of this century when women became less anxious to bear more children. Provence has been particularly rich in folk mythology, beliefs, superstitions, in the use of signs and portents, folk medicine, charms, rituals and sorceries, even down to solemn legal prosecutions of insects when crops have been plagued by caterpillars, locusts or bush-crickets, and this well into the 19th century. Most have died out in favour of the 20th century shibboleths.

After Varages is Tavernes, surely a *taverna* halting-place on a Roman road. On the knoll which bears the hamlet of Fox-Amphoux is the Auberge du Vieux-Fox whose meals are distinguished and original, and bedrooms are minute and quaint. To sit, drink in hand, on the little terrace as the sun sets and pours its last rays on the grave pyramids of the Gros and Petit Bessillon hills, is a moment's suspension in silent contentment. Sillans-la-Cascade is so named on account of the waterfall of the Bresque river. Salernes, also on the Bresque, and rather larger, has fountains, a ruined 13th century castle, and the recommended Hostellerie Allègre. Flayosc, thick-walled and coolly grey, with a steep curving main street, is the last village before Draguignan which administers the Var *département*; its markets are more exciting than its undistinguished monuments. Perhaps the most deserving of these is the Pierre de la Fée, northwest of the town, a perfectly preserved megalithic dolmen of three hugh upright stones supporting a massive capstone, watched over by the three symbolic trees of Provence—the holm oak, juniper, and nettle tree. Druidical ceremonies were held at the Pierre de la Fée until the 5th century A.D.

Draguignan has had various names in the past but all were based on the same Celtic root, *drac*, the dragon who stood for the forces of darkness and fear whose mythology is widespread. The local legend says the *drac* terrorised the land until overpowered by St. Hermentaire, first known bishop of Antibes, whose hermitage is close to Draguignan's outskirts. The legend resembles the better known one in which St. Martha slew the *tarasque* (again the same Celtic root) of the Rhône, and both convey with vivid imagery the triumph of Christianity over paganism.

Equally inviting villages beckon further south. Barjols, a green and watered tanning town, whose houses rise steeply from the banks of two streams (the Hôtel Pont d'Or is inexpensive and suitable for a night); Cotignac at the foot of a tufa hill, its 17th and 18th century houses having been tastefully restored.

And so to our second major river, the Argens. It is a pleasant exercise to follow its course, as far as roads allow. Its source is near Seillons-Source-d'Argens which is not far from St. Maximin whose church is linked with the early history of Christianity in Provence. Tradition has it that Mary Magdalene and Maximinus, the martyred bishop of Aix, and two other saints who had landed at *Li Santo* in the Camargue, are buried here. St. Maximin is an extraordinary church to come upon. Massive, incomplete, a pure Northern Gothic building planted in Provence. To an eye accustomed to Provençal Romanesque, St. Maximin seems out of place. Splendid and austere, yes, but belonging to Provence, hardly. Long before the building was begun in 1295 pilgrims flocked to the site. It was put up after the sarcophagi of the saints had been discovered. The statues of the saints were hacked down during the French Revolution when the town of St. Maximin was renamed Marathon. In the mid-19th century the preacher Lacordaire tried to revive the once famous pilgrimage to the shrine of St. Mary Magdalene, but it was short-lived. Today, the visitor can go down to the tiny crypt to see the casket in its cramped vault. The popular pilgrimage on July 21st and 22nd is to the grotto of the penitent Magdalene high on La Sainte-Baume, and reached by a path through the woodlands once sacred to the Gauls and partly felled by Caesar for his blockade of Marseille.

The fame of Fréjus lies with its Roman monuments. Most of them disappoint because of their degraded state, but they are interesting by virtue of the historical context and the special function of Roman Fréjus. The presence of a theatre, arena, ramparts, towers and aqueducts is nothing unusual in Roman towns of Provence, but the port installations and garrison buildings such as the military laundry, baths, hospital and *palestra* sports ground rouse curiosity.

Julius Caesar founded *Forum Julii* in 49 B.C. as a naval base and staging post, the nearest he could find from which to deal with Marseille, now his enemy. The site was at the edge of a stagnant, malarial lagoon, but was already a Greco-Ligurian town, as was testified by Agricola (40-93 A.D.), conqueror and governor of Britain and the most famous citizen of Fréjus. Caesar's port was built in haste. Later, Agrippa built a larger harbour further west. During 2,000 years silt has pushed back the sea by more than a kilometre, and the Roman harbour lies below the railway line. Roman marine engineers had a constant battle against the silt brought down by the Argens which they had to dredge and canalise into the sea. They had to build a wall to break the force of the *mistral*. But the Roman road, the *Via Aurelia*, could be brought down to the sea once the Oxybian tribe had been pacified, and another road was pushed quickly north to Forcalquier, *Forum Neronis*.

Even during the 1st century A.D. the military value of *Forum Julii* declined. Henry II tried to revive it in the 16th century but it soon fell into decay through silt and malaria. Visigoths and Saracens at separate times destroyed parts of Fréjus. In the 19th century a newer town was built and much Roman material was used. Any building standing today which is at least 150 years old will probably have plenty of Roman fragments in its walls. That *Forum Julii* had been a Roman garrison town is evidenced by the stark buildings, some of them put up in haste by inexperienced workmen—prisoners of war, convicted criminals, soldiers turned builders. Their material was quarried from the porphyry deposits in the Estérel and Maures. They used small bricks which were cheaper and quicker to handle than large blocks. They seized any natural outcrop of rock to save work in erecting the ramparts and arena. Foundations were of rubble, not brick. Here was cost-conscious Rome at work. Utility, not grandeur. The only fairly lavishly ornamented building is *Porta orae*, 'the gate at the border', and not as sometimes wrongly translated as Porte Dorée or 'golden gate'. Other decorative fragments found locally are housed in the museum close to the cloisters, church and 5th century baptistery.

Fifty kilometres north of Fréjus is the village of Mons. From nearby, the Romans tapped the streams and built a series of daring constructions to bring water to *Forum Julii*. Ramblers will come across groups of ruined arches in the countryside. The handsomest are in the grounds of Château Aurélien, outside Fréjus to the northeast, among umbrella pines. This was the longest aqueduct system built by the Romans in southern France, yet it is said that it had not been soundly constructed, for repair work had to be carried out not long after its completion.

10 · EAST OF THE DURANCE

On the east side of the river Durance, between Peyruis and Manosque but on the opposite bank, rises the Plateau de Valensole. It is sparsely populated and frequently dissected by valleys whose streams flow towards the Durance. The only substantial river to cut across the plateau is the Asse, and between it and the river Bléone to the north are few roads, few villages, and almost nothing of consequence to interest the guidebook until you come to Digne, save for the Rochers des Mées. A natural wall of weathered puddingstone which sometimes attains 100 metres above the surrounding ground, it lies near where Durance and Bléone meet. By moonlight, or from a distance, these finger-like cliffs look like a human procession, and they are popularly called *Les Pénitents*. The name Les Mées derives from the Latin *metae*, boundary stones, which these rocks vaguely resemble.

Digne is the administrative capital of the Alpes-de-Haute-Provence. It is a sizeable town of nearly 16,000 inhabitants, and has a fistful of hotels for travellers using the *Route Napoléon*. Some authors write affectionately of Digne, not least the explorer Alexandra David-Neel who died there in 1969 at the age of 101, and found the surrounding country similar to Tibet. Partly surrounded by peaks and cliffs streaked with dark marl and eroded by wind and water whose threatening shapes throw a chill over the town even in sunshine, Digne seems alien to Provence. The feeling is not dispelled by the fact that the majestic Romanesque church of Notre Dame du Bourg, with an alpine influence on its Provençal architecture, is closed. The key has to be hunted for at the cemetery. Digne has a long history, a cathedral, a museum, a thermal establishment for the treatment of rheumatism. It holds an important annual lavender fair at the beginning of September. It has an upper and a lower town, and

Like penitents in procession, Rochers des Mées near the Durance

its Boulevard Gassendi honours the name of a prodigious philosopher of the 17th century whose mind embraced every known branch of knowledge of his time, born at nearby Champtercier. Those glowering mountains, they say, are a stimulating challenge to climbers.

Back in Provence on the Plateau de Valensole, and around the village of that name, the contours seem to have been moulded by a potter's hand which has shaped soft curves out of the light, sand-coloured soil, and decorated each concavity with row on row of precise dots of lavender bushes. Thin and clear, midway between lowlands and alps, the light dances here, and the artist is compelled to use a different range of colours. Almonds, fruit trees, and truffles which, they boast, rival those of Périgord. It is not really olive country up here. But lavender is king, and when it flowers beehives dot the fields. Round the gentle bowl in which Valensole is set, distant ranges poke their pale silhouettes over the rim. The sky is immense.

Valensole is untidy; its streets are steep. You can choose between the smart modern Hôtel Piès on the southern outskirts or the Grand Hôtel in the centre where commercial travellers in a modest line of

Remains of Roman temple to Apollo, Riez

agricultural business stay. Valensole is the birthplace of the unfortunate Admiral Villeneuve who, by losing to Nelson at Trafalgar, ended Napoleon's dream of invading England. No fine memorial for losers.

   A more immediately charming village is Riez, fourteen kilometres to the southeast. It sits coquettishly at the foot of a knoll, and is very ancient. It was an important town, *Reia Apollinaris*, on the Roman road between Grenoble and Fréjus. Its Roman remains are four grey granite Corinthian columns whose architraves and bases are of white marble, all that is left of a temple to Apollo, one may assume. They stand in a neat compound just outside Riez, silently impressive when no-one else is looking at them, a little incongruous when a party of shuffling, half-interested school children under shrill instruction pass in crocodiles. It is extraordinary to reflect that the nearest place where grey granite could have been quarried was at Pennafort near Callas in the Var, 117 kilometres away. In a cramped 5th century baptistery are housed other Roman remains unearthed by the enthusiast, Marcel Provence. Much of *Reia Apollinaris* still lies unexcavated beneath the fields and houses of Riez.

The pleasant valley drive along the Colostre from Riez through Allemagne-en-Provence—named after the fertility goddess Alemona—follows the route of Roman *Via Sixtia* to Aix, along which the produce of the Riez district was carried. On the way lies Gréoux-les-Bains, a staid little spa which the Romans had exploited for treating arthritis. When the Western Roman Empire collapsed, the curative value of the sulphurous waters was forgotten until its rediscovery in the 16th century. In the grounds of the baths are traces of a Roman building and a Roman inscription dedicated to the nymphs of the place, *Nymphis Grisellicis*. Gréoux's name can be traced from *griselium* (*gresum*, pain, and *lin*, water).

Gréoux-les-Bains stands above the river Verdon some kilometres before it joins the Durance. Upstream lie the Gorges du Verdon, by far the most spectacular canyons in Europe. Twenty-one kilometres long, and formed partly by geological folding pressures and partly by the erosion of the river, these closely-set, flat-topped cliffs fall precipitately to where the tiny Verdon worms its way 400 to 700 metres below. Early in this book I said that the spectacular and Provence seemed to me incompatible—for Provence is essentially composed of Mediterranean harmonies. The grandiosely claustrophobic scene lies in Provence but is not of it. The Gorges du Verdon might be anywhere.

They are as well visited from Castellane to the east as from Moustiers-Sainte-Marie to the west. Castellane on the Verdon has a clean

Picturesquely sited Moustiers-Sainte-Marie

charm of old gates and streets and a 12th century church. They lie on the further side of a large and welcoming main square alongside the main through-road. Around the square is a number of small, homely and reasonably-priced hotels. Behind the small town surges a Cyclopean natural keep, a square mass of rock which constantly draws the eyes up its 200 metres. On its flat top is perched a tiny chapel, Notre Dame du Rocher.

Moustiers-Sainte-Marie is strung out halfway up a bare range of jagged rocks. The highly picturesque town is divided by a bridged chasm down which plunges the Rioul stream in a series of cascades. High above, suspended between two pinnacles is a long metal chain with a gilded star of Bethlehem in the middle. This *Chaine de l'Etoile* is commonly supposed to have been put there—though goodness knows how—by the troubadour Baron de Blacas as an *ex voto* after his release from prison following the battle of Damietta during the Seventh Crusade in 1249. During the 17th and 18th centuries, Moustiers rose to fame for its fine porcelain. The best pieces are sought by collectors the world over, and examples are to be seen in the town's faïence museum, as well as in museums in Marseille and Aix. During the same centuries, Marseille, Apt, Avignon and Varages were also producing high quality faïence. At Moustiers, four distinct phases of style can be traced, each arising under the influence of a different master potter. The best work was of delicate and graceful polychrome arabesques painted on a milk-white glaze. It was exported far and wide. A million pieces a year were sent to the great fair at Beaucaire, either by cart, or more riskily in order to get there quickly, by boat along the turbulent Durance. In the 19th century the industry died out, to be revived in 1926 by the great benefactor Marcel Provence. What is sold in the shops is not always of the finest quality.

Now to the Gorges du Verdon. The river itself has undergone major changes in recent years with the construction of barrages, one near Gréoux, the second at Sainte-Croix. The reservoir of the latter is the largest in France, and in one year looked as though it was a natural and not a man-made phenomenon. In drowning the valley and some villages, the engineers had to put a splendid Roman bridge over the Verdon near Aiguines under the waters. What one crosses by now is more convenient but a great deal more prosaic.

The tourist road known as the *Corniche Sublime* follows the southern edge of the gash which is the Gorges du Verdon, to provide plummetting and vertiginous views. Among the vantage places are the Balcons de la Mescla, Pont de l'Artuby where the Artuby gorges enter those of the Verdon, Falaise des Cavaliers near which is a monument to the first explorers of the gorge in 1905—Isadore Blanc, Abbé Pascal, and the indefatigable pioneer of speleology who opened up hundreds of caves in France, E.A. Martel—or the Col d'Illoire. On the north side, a circuit can be made round the Belvédères de la Maline, while experienced walkers can descend to the Sentier Martel from the Chalet de la Maline, to cover some fifteen kilometres near the river bed.

South of the Verdon gorges is an extensive, denuded region of hard limestone plateaux, the Grands Plans, which, like the Plateau de Vaucluse, resisted the mountain-folding processes which had created the Verdon chasm. The largest area, the Grand Plan de Canjuers, slopes towards the lowlands, and then drops to a sharp escarpment behind Draguignan. The lower altitudes are called the *pays d'en bas*. The Grand Plan de Canjuers is a military zone which means that various roads are shut and some villages had to be abandoned—not without strenuous protest. The road from La Bastide, through Comps-sur-Artuby and along the *Corniche Sublime* follows the northern margin of the prohibited zone. Two roads are permanently open through the zone: between Comps and Montferrat, and between Bargeme and Bargèmon. The southern boundary is followed by the road between Châteaudouble and Saint-Andrieux. There is no danger of straying; the Keep Out notices are ubiquitous.

A string of medieval villages look down from their erstwhile fastnesses towards the olives and warmth of the Mediterranean not far away below them. A few years ago the life of these little populations, walled in those tall, grey, rampart-like houses and narrow streets, was ebbing away. There was no economic life to sustain them. They looked and felt a little like the decaying monasteries of the Greek Meteora. Now, revived by tourism and the French passion for the *résidence secondaire*, many are letting in fresh winds, expanding with modern villas beyond the old villages, and the medieval houses are refurbished, and there are hotels and restaurants. New-old Tourtour, for instance, fashionable and with a coppery vista of the Estérel and Maures; Ampus, unfairly neglected by most guide-books, where the abbé has painted the Stations of the Cross on fourteen tile-panels let into the rock going up to the *castrum*; the 13th century chapel at Comps-sur-Artuby; or walled-in Bargème. I imagine that if I could look through the archives of Figanières I would find entries to show how its wealth in the past came from the growing and selling of figs. Both Callas and Bargemon have interesting things to see in their churches; Seillans, perhaps one of the most delightful of all these villages; Fayence rather larger than the rest; Tourrettes and Callian both dominated by castles; and finally Montauroux, the last village in Var and close to where the Alpes-Maritimes begin. All these places are reached by lovely, winding, secondary roads.

There is one more village, by the odd name of Aups, for which I feel affection not only because of its fountains fed by springs rising in the fissured limestone hills around the open plateau in which Aups lies, but also for the story behind its name. Aups is known for its honey, but it seems to have another and curious claim to fame. Some books relate that Julius Caesar had said he would sooner be the first man in Aups than the second in Rome. An improbable story, even supposing Aups existed in Caesar's time, but how it gained currency was quickly elucidated for me by the classicist, the late Professor Harold Harris. The Greek historian Plutarch in his *Life of Caesar*—written well over a century after Caesar's death—recorded that while Caesar was crossing the Alps on his way to Spain, he passed a small and miserable barbarian village. At this point the great general had proclaimed "he preferred the first place in that to the second in Rome," in illustration of a facet of Caesar's character. Aups came to be identified with this 'miserable village' because its name derives from old Provençal *aupiho* or 'little alp' (as in Alpilles), with an even older pre-Roman, Celto-Ligurian root of *alb* ('hill pasture'), a word absorbed into both Latin and Greek. Plutarch wrote in Greek; when he speaks of Caesar "crossing the Alps" (*Alpeis*), only a little word-twisting was later called for to interpret the phrase as Caesar 'crossing by Aups'. Who perpetrated this small semantic deceit is not known. To me, a possible candidate with a vested interest in bringing immortality to Aups could have been the Abbé Jean in the 18th century. I only hope I do not besmirch his name with false innuendo. He built himself a house in Aups. Being a man of encyclopaedic knowledge, he erected in his garden a column on which he carved a summary of all human knowledge to the year 1760; he made, too, an extraordinary globe, a sundial and a moondial. Indoors, on the tiled floor he constructed a map of Europe based on his astronomical calculations which proved that the centre of Europe was indubitably—Aups.

11 · THE RIVIERA

From Les Saintes-Maries-de-la-Mer to Menton on the Italian frontier is the coastline of the French Riviera, a southward bulging curve of great diversity. Its fame as a magnet to summer visitors dates only from the last fifty years or so. The adoration of sun and sea has been the expression of an emancipation from the previous constraints when the world's social élite was in residence during a winter season governed by formal conventions. That season was enjoyed at Cannes, Nice, Menton and Monte-Carlo that made up the classical Côte d'Azur, a name invented by the novelist Stéphen Liégeard in 1887.

Climate determines much of human behaviour, and so it can take priority in a discussion about resorts and beaches. At smaller resorts along the coast the summer season is surprisingly short. Many hotels do not open until early May and close again towards the end of September. Larger towns like Nice have a summer and winter season, as well as out-of-season tourism with comparatively low-priced package arrangements for business and professional congresses at the larger hotels.

The brevity of the season is due in part to conservative French habits in relation to school holiday periods, and in part—and paradoxically—to the Mediterranean climate. For many the ideal temperatures of both beach and water coincide with the children's holidays in July and August. May and June may be fine but the water has yet to warm up after winter; moreover, the clearer the day the greater the radiation at sunset when the temperature drops markedly, to rise again after dusk and set the nocturnal crickets singing. Even in midsummer days are shorter than they are further north (while round the winter solstice they are somewhat longer). In the south they say summer begins to take its leave on August 25th, so that later on in September and early October, however fine the weather, a feeling of enclosing autumn falls upon the resorts. Out of the high season air and water may feel relatively cool, especially along exposed parts of the coast.

Exposed to what? it may be asked. Mainly the *mistral* which can blow for a few hours or days at any time of the year when low pressure systems over the western Mediterranean draw colder central European air down the funnel of the Rhône. Surface temperatures of the sea are lowered quickly; beaches can be made stingingly uncomfortable. The *mistral* swings eastwards along the coast and lashes any place without hill protection to north and west. This is precisely why the 'old' Riviera, the Côte d'Azur between Menton and La Napoule acquired its 19th century popularity (and for retired Roman officials 2,000 years ago), and why the oldest of all southern French winter resorts, Hyères, fell from favour. The same insufficient protection empties St. Tropez in winter. The high amphitheatre of the Maritime Alps and Estérel bar central Europe's winter from the Côte d'Azur which is far enough away from the Rhône valley for the *mistral* to have spent itself. A few meteorological figures show the trend. At Avignon, the mean January temperature is 4.1° C.; at Marseille, 6.3°; at Nice, 8.4°; at Menton, 9.3°. In July, the trend is

St. Tropez and its gulf

almost reversed. Avignon (24.1° C.) is hotter than Marseille (22.3°) and Nice (21.9°) and the same as Menton, when the sea's temperature is lower than the land's. Menton is the warmest place along the French Mediterranean coast, its natural mountain barrier radiating heat back into the Mentonese basin, its position facing snugly southeast. More than once, in June or September, have we driven from a cold, wet, blustery Var coast to find at Menton a warmth in process of driving rainclouds upwards to evaporation.

Let it not be said that only the English talk about the weather. In the south of France the topic is usually under serious consideration, never more so than when exceptional heat, cold, rain or drought threaten the visitor's well-being. *Ce n'est pas normal*, the locals incredulously conclude. The weather, I think, is never normal. Its vagaries are endless and fascinating. Prediction of the day's weather pattern is made with caution. It requires uncanny skill to read those quickly boiling clouds and contrary winds. If a gentle breeze follows the rising of the sun, then that day will remain fine.

Older inhabitants of the Riviera say their climate is changing for the worse. Memories of yesteryear play one false, perhaps, but world climatic patterns are altering, the meteorologists say. Cyclonic or anticyclonic conditions move away less rapidly, are less quickly replaced by another weather pattern, and mean annual temperatures are falling imperceptibly. If one reads the older literature about the Riviera, the impression of a perpetually splendid climate dominates. Before the 1914-18 war most people spent a whole winter, from October to May, on the Côte d'Azur. To have stayed on to face the dreadful heat of summer along with the natives was unthinkable. In seven months, whatever rain or cold there was, was relegated to its proper time-proportions. Today, a few days of indifferent weather in a fortnight's holiday are remembered as thieves of treasured possessions.

The Mediterranean climate is not a gentle one. Its transitions are fierce and uncompromising. Midsummer thunder-storms are sudden, short, of tropical intensity. Streets are instantly awash; dry gulleys become incontinent torrents that spew their booty of rocks, trees or dead cats out to sea in widening arcs of dirty brown. Drystone walls, patiently built over the centuries to conserve precious soil, are breached. In drought, soil cracks and leaves shrivel; trees are ignited by a careless match to start the fearful conflagrations which are the annual scourge of the Riviera hillsides. Seasons come and go with startling abruptness.

The boat for Corsica leaves Nice harbour

Curious how it nonetheless remains the notion of an ideal climate, an inspiration to painter and poet, the inducement for the northerner's annual migration to the sun. It is capable of matchless perfection. From May to the first days of October its invigorating warmth teases out the scent of hot pine-resin, of broom and aromatic herbs. The first autumn rains regenerate the parched ground and germinate the dormant seeds. October is a kind of little spring. In April come the true spring rains followed by the full flowering of thousands of plants which die back by June. From June to September is a kind of winter when most things sleep.

The surface heat of the sea does not quite synchronise with the seasons. Its temperature drops during the winter and is slow to reheat, but it retains its summer heat until well into the cooler days of autumn. Not that the Mediterranean sea, whose tides hardly exceed one metre, is ever really cold. It is a deep sea in which the immense weight of water creates its own warmth. After the *mistral* has chilled the surface enough to drive away the swimmers, rising thermals quickly reheat it.

January is often the loveliest winter month. Humidity is low and brings startling clarity and intensity of colour. The best photographs are taken then. It can be cold, but the air is as heady as wine, pure and 'elastic' (the word used about the air of Nice by Tobias Smollett, over two centuries ago). Mimosa trees explode a scented, fluffy yellow across the land, and oranges shine, lantern bright, from among their deep green, glittering leaves. Every ten years or so, on average, the cold European winter is pushed over the mountain ridges by the *gregaou* wind, and olive and lemon trees suffer damage. Even at Menton a thin film of snow lies for a day or two. In recent years hard winters have come in 1940-41, 1955-56, 1962-63 and 1970-71. *Ce n'est pas normal.* A couple of times in a century really hard winters invade inland Provence and the coast. That of 1955-56 was tremendously destructive of fruit trees; the weight of snow smashed greenhouses at Antibes.

A few private beaches, part of estates which run down to the sea, are concentrated on once-fashionable promontories and indented sections of coast. Most beaches are free to all, although parts of some are leased to entrepreneurs who hire out parasols, mattresses, chairs or pedalos, and give swimming or sailing instructions. Buoys mark

Calanque de Sormiou, a drowned valley near Marseille

the limits within which motorboats and water-skiers may not approach.

Because its physical features are so varied, the diversity of the Riviera coast is striking. There are intimate coves, long open beaches of shingle, pebbles or fine sand—sometimes silicious, sometimes calcareous. Expanses of sand are not to be compared with the ribbons of Languedoc, but the choice is ample. The long spit of dune-backed sands outside Les Saintes-Maries-de-la-Mer, reached by the rough track of the *Digue de la Mer*; the curving bay of Les Lecques; the gentle inclines at Hyères, Le Lavandou, Cavalaire, Pampelonne south of St. Tropez, Ste. Maxime, St. Aygulf and Fréjus-Plage separated by the mouth of the River Argens, Cannes and Juan-les-Pins. St. Raphaël, too, has its sands, and also utilises sand, sea water, marine plants and algae for the comparatively new thalassotherapy used for treating arthritic conditions.

By contrast, there are the little coves belonging to fishing villages turned modest resorts at Carro, Sausset-les-Pins, or Carry-le-Rouet at the foot of the Chaîne de l'Estaque west of Marseille. Or the enclosed bays of La Fossette, Aiguebelle or Rayol along the Corniches des Maures. Agay, Anthéor and Le Trayas are sheltered by the deep red rocks of the Estérel. Cassis is tucked into the apex of its bight, towered over by the 399 metres of Cap Canaille, the highest coastal cliff in France. To the west of Cassis are the sunken limestone valleys of the Calanques, approached only by boat or on foot. To look down on the slopes and hills towards Cassis from the Marseille road on a September evening when a purple glow suffuses sky, sea and land is a spectacle the eye does not forget.

If the coastline is varied, so is the immediate hinterland. What could offer a greater contrast than the Camargue behind Les Saintes-Maries-de-la-Mer and the rocks that hang over Beaulieu? Bandol, Sanary, Bormes-les-Mimosas, St Tropez, Cros-de-Cagne and Menton all come to mind as places whose immediate inland countryside is a delight to explore. Some (though not all) of the recently built places have grace and distinction. I think particularly of Port Grimaud, a little Provençal Venice of canals and footpaths, built out into the Golfe de St. Tropez, where gaiety and lightness has been added to houses in traditional styles. Some building developments are an offence against the environment: tall blocks have spoiled the once simple charm of Le Lavandou; the skyline of Monaco has come to resemble a diminutive New York; the islet of Bendor has hotels in doubtful taste; even staid Menton has ravaged its good looks with

Monaco, the modern skyline and the Larvotto beach

unworthy buildings up its five radiating valleys. Yet the Promenade des Anglais in Nice still impresses by the sweeping magnitude of its seafront boulevards, and La Croisette in Cannes by its undimmed elegance. In total contrast is Port-Cros, the middle and smallest of the three Iles d'Hyères, the 'Golden Isles', where the natural vegetation and unusual bird life have been conserved since 1963 when the island was declared a National Park.

Of course, too many areas have been overbuilt and overloaded with marinas and cementscapes. Yet I find that discretion has come out pretty well against rapacity and exploitation and the universal eyesore of the motor car.

The eastern arm of the wide bay of Hyères is formed by Cap Bénat and possesses the least disturbed, pristine stretch of coastline between the Spanish and Italian frontiers. My wife and I have been returning to this little *pays* just over the hill from Le Lavandou for many years. Familiarity has in no way diminished its power to act as balm of regenerative inspiration. Here, an outcrop of tree-covered Maures hills slopes towards the sea. The flatter surfaces are either left to nature's holm oaks, cork oaks and *maquis* shrubs, or else they are cultivated with vineyard rows which point towards the setting sun and reach almost as far as the sand dunes and maritime pines that announce the sea on the further side. At certain spots along the little road are visions of the intense blue sea framed by vines, trees, a corner of a bay, and the arrowhead hills beyond Hyères. The land is owned and worked by a number of large estates. Some bays and beaches are private, but the curving sandy beach of Brégançon is free. At one end the handsome Fort de Bregançon, owned by the State, stands on guard. Sunsets are Turnerian. At l'Estagnol, where twisted pines throw contorted shadows across the silver-sanded beach, you pay to enter. On the horizon float the Iles d'Hyères. In high summer, cicadas rasp away above one's head in the trees. An occasional yacht glides into the bay. No building is visible, only the ring of dark trees and rising rocks at each end of the shallow Estagnol bay. True, military aircraft and helicopters from Hyères sweep and clatter overhead, and on summer Sundays the beach is full and the air redolent of 'Ambre Solaire'. I know no beach anywhere in the south of France, open to the public, to compare with l'Estagnol.

Cannes and the Estérel range

I write about this corner of the Maures only after an inner debate. The temptation is to cling to the illusion that the discovery we had made when few people ever came this way (for there was not even a proper road) is a private possession. We all try to preserve a paradise garden. Such secretiveness is illogical, all the more so as I played a small part in getting the only hotel in the vicinity into the bible for travellers in France, the *Guide Michelin*. Hôtel Les Palmiers at Cabasson has an entry in red (for its delightful position) and is there for all who buy the guide to inspect. Cabasson is a hamlet, a kilometre from the seashore, without shops or church, surrounded by country, wine *domaines*, and silence at night. There is nothing remarkable about the modern buildings of the hotel which was originally in an old Provençal house a few metres away—a place of character and some inconvenience—until it became too small. Les Palmiers is a pension for those who speak French, seek no entertainment beyond what the environment supplies, and accept the French holiday habit of turning out all the lights by nine-thirty when everything falls asleep.

This is the last piece of almost unmolested coast. If Joseph Conrad were writing *The Rover* today instead of in the 1920's he could have come to Cabasson without surprise. The integrity of the *pays* is maintained, I suspect, by the vigilance of the private and influential landlords. I never expected to be grateful for such a benign exercise of power.

12 · IN AND AROUND MARSEILLE

A hyphen often divides Marseille from Aix to indicate a growing urban-industrial agglomeration. The countryside between them is more congested than it was when John Evelyn wrote in his *Diary* on leaving Aix for Marseille in 1644:

From hence Octob: 7 we had a most delicious journey to Marselles through a Country, sweetely declining to the South & Mediterranean Coasts, full of Vineyards, & Olive-yards, Orange trees, Myrtils, Pomegranads & the like sweete Plantations, to which belong innumerable pleasantly situated Villas, ...

Marseille is an intellectual, commercial and industrial centre. Above all, it is France's major port, for long known as 'the gateway to the Orient', and now, in changing circumstances, turning more towards Europe, and spreading westwards to ensure its links with oil depots and refineries. Martigues, once one of the most picturesque fishing villages along the coast, lies between Marseille and the oil port of Lavéra, and is becoming hemmed in by industrialisation. Martigues, whose tricolor flag was adopted by the French Revolution, faces over the salt-brilliant Etang de Berre whose shores still offer engaging views: near Istres and St. Mitre-les-Remparts, and the early Greek settlement of St. Blaise whose magnificent military walls can be inspected close to.

Marseille is spreading in other directions, too; towards Allauch on the flank of the white Garlaban peak, 'the white hill', so named by Phoenicians from the Hebrew *Gabaa-laban*; into the *calanques* at Luminy where an ambitious university centre is forming; it is urbanism all the way to Aubagne.

The ordinary traveller will either miss out Marseille altogether or

Fisherman mending his net, Vallon des Auffes, Marseille

else dig in and get to know it. For the latter, there is much that is worthwhile. The former will at least savour the vitality and the restaurants, walk along the Canebiere, the main street whose name derives from *cannabis*, hemp, for this used to be the street of the rope traders. He will be drawn to the Vieux-Port, still picturesque, and perhaps take the most popular of all excursions, the boat trip to the Château d'If. Its 16th century fortifications are heavily encrusted with the patina of the *Count of Monte Cristo*, Alexandre Dumas' fantastic and evergreen yarn, written in 1844-45, whose characters are treated as real on the Château d'If.

The Count of Mont Cristo's Château d'If

Back in Marseille, there are shopping streets, a few bits of Vieux Marseille in the Panier quarter, some handsome 18th century mansions in Rue Sainte. Most churches are unattractive, though the onetime cathedral of the 12th century is an exception, and two hilltop churches provide grandstand views of sea, hills and port installations. It is no good asking to see where the *Marseillaise* was written. Rouget de Lisle wrote a song called *Chant de guerre pour l'Armée du Rhin* in Strasbourg on April 25th 1792. Later that year, 600 fanatical volunteers from Marseille were called on to march on Paris in the bloody revolutionary days; they adopted Rouget de Lisle's song and renamed it *La Marseillaise*.

There are museums to satisfy diverse interests. I choose the Beaux-Arts at the top of the handsome flight of steps and in Palais Longchamp. Many different European schools of painting, from the 15th to 18th centuries are represented, as well as those minor landscapists that preceded and followed Cézanne, all of whom add their painterly

Marseille from the Palais Longchamp steps

explanation of the Provençal landscape. Especially noteworthy are the Marseille-born artists, such as Honoré Daumier, the superb draughtsman whose pen and brush commented ceaselessly on the social and political scene; Pierre Puget, one of the greatest French sculptors; Adolphe Monticelli; François Granet; Gustave Ricard; Charles Camoin, Cézanne's friend. Four canvases by one artist hold me longest. They are the only known paintings by the 18th century woman artist, Françoise Duparc. Part of her fairly short life was spent in England where she painted and exhibited, but these works have vanished. In the Beaux-Arts are four anonymous portraits of humble people, painted with delicate restraint, subtlety, with such poise and modesty and inner quiet that every feeling of compassion and admiration is aroused.

Other paintings are housed in the Musée Grobet-Labadie, as well as furniture and tapestries; Musée Cantini specialises in modern art and temporary exhibitions, and a section is the Musée de la faïence.

The archaeologist comes off best. He can come face to face with the earliest Christian worship in Provence in the catacombs below the Basilica of Saint Victor. Roman Marseille has been open to the public since 1963 with the Musée des Docks romains, 28 Place Vivaux, near the Hôtel de Ville. Among the exhibits are the Roman docks and huge *dolia* storage jars in their original position. A wreck, discovered by Jacques Cousteau near the islet of Grand Congloué, of a ship from Delos which had foundered between 150 and 130 B.C. is of particular interest as I shall refer to it again towards the end of the next chapter in connection with an excursion from Menton.

Until recently, finds relating to Marseille's Greek past were single objects and not structural. During reconstruction work behind the Bourse in 1967, ramparts, quays and fortifications erected by the Phocaeans have been exposed. They date from the 3rd and 2nd centuries B.C., thus some 300 years after the founding of *Massalia*. Now, the position and extent of *Massalia* can be accurately identified. These are the defensive walls which were besieged by Julius Caesar's lieutenants in 49 B.C. with assault towers, missiles and rams, and from which the Phocaeans—the pedlars of the Mediterranean, they have been called—fired mangonels and javelins from catapults, and set fire to the Roman revetments.

A knowledge of regional archaeology is enriched at Musée Borély, an 18th century château in a park. In the Salle de Roquepertuse the finds from the Gallic sanctuary near Rognac are displayed. The whole portico—3rd to 2nd century B.C.—has been reconstructed.

No wonder the Romans regarded the Saluvii as barbaric and ferocious; the skulls of enemy heads severed in battle adorn the portico's niches. When the head had been cut off in battle it was carried at the saddle—the soul of the dead being carried to the next world. At the top of the portico is a carved bird. A simple and impressively incised frieze of horses' heads is also on show, as are two statues of heroes squatting cross-legged in the so-called Buddha position which Gallic warriors adopted, the lotus-leaf posture of eternal repose. How recognisably modern are the carved faces of some of these Celto-Ligurians whose drooping moustaches seem to hide an enigmatic pursing of the lips.

Amid the commercial clangour of the city, they hold a delightful (though no doubt perfectly commercial) fair between December 10th and January 4th, the *Foire aux santons*. *Santons* are the small clay figurines made at Aubagne of brightly painted village folk of Provence, usually dressed in yesteryear's costumes and accompanied by the tools of their trade. Street vendors, fishermen, poachers, musicians, policemen, all are placed at Christmas time in the crib along with the classical figures associated with the Nativity. The Christmas crib is an essential part of Provençal celebrations. The prominence given to these homely, secular *santons*, which may have originated in

Santons, painted clay figurines essential to a Provençal Christmas

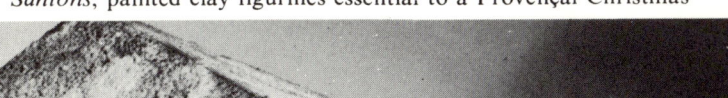

Italy in the 14th century, indicates how strongly Mediterranean realism influenced Christianity in Provence. Here is a happy preoccupation with birth, the unfolding of life, and with the imagery of human contact, a microcosm of village life as it once was. Compare this outlook with the withdrawn asceticism of the medieval world, of inland Cistercian Provence, or with the obsession with death in the religious outlook of present-day Brittany.

How much of the traditional Christmas is observed now in Provence is hard to say, but the pattern used to begin with the planting of grains of wheat in saucers on December 4th, St. Barbara's Day. Just before Christmas comes the careful preparation of the crib. The figurines are placed in their proper positions. The crib is decorated with greenery, pebbles, twigs, moss and the bark of trees. On Christmas Eve the family gathers round the *Cacho-fiò*, the Yule log of olive, almond or cherry wood. A glass of unfermented wine is poured over the flaming log, and a traditional Provençal song is sung. Dinner follows, and is likely to consist of garlic soup, cardoons (akin to globe artichokes), snails previously gathered and at table pricked out with an acacia thorn and eaten with the splendid garlic mayonnaise, *aïoli*. Eels may be served next, and salad. Thirteen desserts are placed on the table: a variety of fruits and nuts, Montélimar nougat, and *fougasse*, the aniseed-flavoured bread, thinly rolled and folded into a criss-cross pattern. Wines are drunk with the meal, finishing with the one first used to sprinkle over the Yule log.

Aubagne, where the *santons* are made, is an uninteresting town where the French Foreign Legion's headquarters are now established after the French withdrawal from Algeria; a museum of the Legion's history is attached to the camp. A little north of Aubagne, on a minor road leading towards the Massif de la Ste Baume, is the hamlet of St. Jean-de-Garguier. In the old priory's chapel is one of the best collections of ex-votos in Provence. There must be a good 200, the oldest dated 1500, an art gallery of primitive pictorial thanks-offerings for death narrowly averted, for health restored, a child safely delivered; expressions of relief from sufferings and anxieties to which man is heir. They are both touching and historically interesting. At one time St. Jean-de-Garguier was a popular place of pilgrimage, and some of the pilgrims performed a curious rite of exorcism by blowing on little clay trumpets. These are still made in Aubagne and still sold in Marseille on St. John's Day. This ancient pagan ritual was practised elsewhere in Provence, and heaps of little discarded trumpets have been unearthed from prehistoric *oppida*.

In the Massif de la Ste. Baume is a chasm by the name of Gouffre de Gaspard de Besse, Provence's Robin Hood in the 18th century. He became legendary while alive, a latter-day demi-god. He was born in the delightful village of Besse in central Var where water flows copiously on each side of its streets, for there is abundant water from a willow-lined lake, the only natural lake I know of in Lower Provence. Gaspard, born in 1757 to a respectable market-gardening family, became well versed in the classics, but took early to banditry, excited by stories of escaping convicts from the fearful galleys of Toulon. Contemporary accounts say he was good looking, dressed with elegance, behaved with great gallantry to the ladies and immense bravado towards men. He fancied himself as a gourmet and was what we would now call a compulsive gambler. Those who supported him praised his every escapade. The women of all ranks wept at his death. His headquarters were the notorious Auberge des Adrets in the Estérel (it is still there but was restored in 1898), and operated mainly in the Gorges d'Ollioules between Toulon and Le Beausset. He became politically important. The peasants were for him, for he helped the poor. He styled himself as the 'enemy of Parliament', a popular slogan since the Parliament of Aix was regarded as a scourge. The aristocracy admired his gallantry and loyalty to his companions. The judges at Aix took a less romantic view of Gaspard; they accused him of numerous murders. When he was finally caught in 1781 he was sentenced to be broken at the wheel. Highway robbery went on into the 19th century. Some of the bandits round Nice were members of the best families there, and lived handsomely off their plunder, inviting the unsuspecting authorities of the town to banquets paid for by their crimes.

13 · ALPINE VALLEYS AND AZUR COAST

East of the Estérel near La Napoule lies the Siagne plain which surrounds Cannes. Beyond are the last outcrops of the Alps which stream like an eager herd of wild beasts down towards their Mediterranean waterhole. This north-south folding of the alpine system has protectively fixed climate, flora and fauna, and human history of the Côte d'Azur. It has given that coastal strip of a mere seventy road-kilometres a backcloth of snow-capped peaks, and their ski slopes, at nearly 3,000 metres above the sea, an arctic circle eighty kilometres from the palm-fringed warmth of Cannes, Antibes, Nice, Cap Ferrat, Beaulieu, Monaco and Menton. It has provided the spectacular excursions through the *clues* or gorges gnawed by alpine torrents—Vésubie, Tinée, Daluis, Cians and Loup are but some—whose valleys lead to an alpine world where the marked footpaths, the *Sentiers de Grande Randonnée*, allow the hardier ones to walk from Nice to Holland. The coast itself has a dramatic geography; picturesque medieval villages such as Eze, Ste-Agnés and Roquebrune command the proud heights that plunge abruptly into the sea.

The sheltered warmth ideally suits the many imported exotic plants and trees. Here, the fruits of bananas, grapefruit, avocado pears, date palms can ripen. Even the familiar olive, eucalyptus, orange, lemon, prickly pear, agave, mimosa and bougainvillea were imported strangers once.

Flowers are cultivated intensively. Immense quantities of roses, jasmin, Seville orange and a host of other scented flowers, gathered in season, are needed by the perfume factories of Grasse. Others supply the cut-flower industry. A few years ago it was a delight to visit the Nice flower market in Cours Saleya, now removed to a new building near the airport. Tobias Smollett had described the despatch of

I.B.M. research centre at Le Gaude near Vence

cut flowers to England in the 18th century, but it was the Parisian journalist, Alphonse Karr, a century later, who put the business on a successful footing with skilled publicity and high prices. He settled at St. Raphaël, inviting the first musicians to come south (Gounod composed *Romeo and Juliet* there in 1866). It has been said that Karr was a misogynist, but he nonetheless had a tumultuous affair with the Provençal novelist, Louise Colet who once stabbed him in the back with a kitchen knife; Karr had it framed and hung on the wall.

For the English, the Riviera's rise to fame is equated with Lord Brougham who, forced by quarantine regulations to stay in Cannes in 1834, settled there and encouraged his aristocratic friends to do likewise. In fact, even before Smollett's famous stay in Nice, small groups of English lived in Nice, since Nice belonged then to the king of Sardinia who, with the English, was at war with France. The famous Promenade des Anglais was so named after the English chaplain, the Rev. Lewis Way who had organised the construction of a coastal path to give work to the peasants whose livelihood had been destroyed by the disastrous winter of 1822. But certainly, after Lord Brougham the coast was transformed from huddles of villages of peasant-fishermen to little towns which learned to cater for outlandish tastes. Gamblers at Monte-Carlo followed, and sedate winter sojourners for whom the seal of respectability was placed by Queen Victoria's visits to the Côte d'Azur. With the post-1918 world came the first sunlovers.

Tourism may appear to be the only industry known to the Côte d'Azur; in reality, science, art, learning, commerce and industry flourish alongside tourism. Since 1965 Nice has had a university with faculties of medicine, science, law and letters, as well as study centres for language, art, drama and music. Cap d'Ail's *Centre Méditerrannéen Universitaire* has an open air theatre. The I.B.M. research centre at La Gaude is of architectural interest. A whole new industrial-academic research complex is being built at Sophia-Antipolis outside Valbonne. On Cap d'Antibes is Villa Thuret, the agronomic research station for Provence. Marine biological research is conducted at Villefranche. There are plant and insect research centres at Menton. Best known of all is Monaco's Musée Océanographique, founded in 1906 by Prince Albert I, and now directed by Jacques Cousteau. In addition to its live exhibits of marine flora and fauna, it has an important research department. Culturally, almost every town has an artistic festival of some kind; of these, the August chamber music festival at Menton is reported in the international press.

Before all these sophisticated activities were evolved, early travellers on their way to imbibe Italian culture on the Grand Tour were entranced by the physical beauty of Menton in particular. Lord Byron was reminded of paradise; Thomas Carlyle of Delphi, calling the hills behind Menton "sacred". In the 1920s Katharine Mansfield more than once referred to Menton as a jewel. From the end of the last century writers, artists and musicians flocked to the coast for its climate and inspiration. Some streets in Nice are still spoken of as *le quartier des musiciens*, though it is long since Berlioz, Meyerbeer, Paganini, Offenbach, Liszt and Stravinsky composed there.

Monaco: Oceanographic Museum
directed by Jacques Cousteau

The artistic invasion continues. The famous shed lustre on towns and villages everywhere. Many a dying hill-village has been resuscitated by painters, potters, wood-carvers and writers. The Côte d'Azur has become a Mecca of modern art through the diversity of its many museums.

Modern painting was implanted in the last century at St. Tropez (then a little fishing village which, even in the 18th century was frowned on as a place where people did not take work seriously). Paul Signac, already famous as a leader of the Neo-Impressionists, sailed his yacht into the Gulf of St. Tropez in 1892. He stayed, painted, and persuaded his friends and colleagues to do the same. Appropriately, the outstanding Musée de l'Annonciade in St. Tropez pays tribute to these pioneers by a splendid collection of their work, not least to Signac himself, even though his divisionist theories and techniques were really at odds with the unitary influence of southern light.

From then on every artist of stature has painted on the Provençal Riviera, and each of three giants who lived and painted on the Côte d'Azur has a museum to himself—Renoir, Matisse and Picasso.

Auguste Renoir was ordered south by his doctors on account of

Henri Matisse's Chapelle du Rosaire at Vence

his progressively crippling arthritis. He built the Domaine des Collettes at Cagnes in 1908 and worked there until his death in 1919, producing those supple, enamelled, sensuous nudes and joyful scenes that seem to have no knowledge of the artist's physical misery. In the museum are only a few works, but there is his studio and wheelchair and a few personal belongings, and the peaceful garden of olive trees.

Henri Matisse settled in the south in 1918, anchoring himself there for the rest of his life, until 1954. The light of Nice was for him a daily miracle. He, too, suffered ill-health towards the end. In gratitude for the nursing he received from the Dominican Order he created the Chapelle du Rosaire in 1950 on the outskirts of Vence, an austere harmony of black and white. On white tiles Matisse painted the black outline of St. Dominic, the Virgin and Child, and the fourteen Stations of the Cross. He designed the rosy-mauve windows. "I want," he said, "those who enter my chapel to feel themselves purified and relieved of their burdens".

In 1963 the Musée Henri Matisse was opened in Villa des Arènes in Nice's suburb of Cimiez. It traces the prodigiously experimental evolution of Matisse's art towards the final phase of limpid gaiety and apparent simplicity which he had drawn from the atmosphere about him.

Pablo Picasso, much of his long life associated with the south of France, is splendidly honoured in the handsome Château des Grimaldi at Antibes. Paintings, drawings, ceramics, sculptures, lithographs done by him during a short period at Antibes and Vallauris, are his joyful salute to Mediterranean light and mythology. On the floor above is a collection of paintings by artists who have lived on the Riviera.

At Vallauris, where Picasso learned his pottery and revitalised the village, are two memorials to the most inventive artist of our time who assimilated every experimental style and those of other civilisations to transmute them with his own restless genius. In the village square stands Picasso's bronze *Man with sheep*, and in the crypt of the 13th century one-time Prieuré de Lérins is his huge *War and peace* fresco.

In contrast, the Musée Fernand Léger outside Biot is incongruous. Léger drew no inspiration from the south, and he said, "I shall never go to the Midi. I loathe it. There is too much sun". Yet shortly before he died in 1955 he bought the plot of land on which his widow had the large museum built. Visible from a long way off, its wide

Potter at Vallauris; an industry revitalised by Pablo Picasso

facade is more than half filled with Léger's largest work, a polychrome mosaic. Inside, an impressive collection of this northern urban machine-artist, a polished, large-scale, monolithic and brash craftsman, is assembled. The art reputation of the Côte d'Azur may be heightened by the presence of the museum but not through any affinity with the environment.

Marc Chagall, who has long lived at Vence, opened the Mémorial Chagall in Cimiez in 1973 when he was aged eighty-six. (Why do artists who work in France live so long?) This Biblical Message Museum houses all his biblical works, and the main exhibits are his seventeen biblical message paintings. A large mosaic by him, *Le Retour d'Ulysse*, is in the Faculty of Laws in Nice.

At Menton, Villefranche, Cap d'Ail and near Fréjus are examples of the facile and neutered works of Jean Cocteau. In Villa Fiesole in Cannes are 100 paintings by Jean-Gabrielle Domergue, pupil of Degas, and recorder of the *folle époque* of the 1920s and 1930s with dashing and sugary young ladies much in evidence.

Permanent exhibitions of high quality can be seen in the Grimaldi château at Cagnes-sur-Mer (which houses also a very interesting olive museum); at Menton's municipal museum; the Musée Jules Chéret in Nice; at the Auberge de la Colombe d'Or in St. Paul where, for the price of a drink, you can see on the walls works by Bonnard, Braque, Derain, Dufy, Matisse, Utrillo and Vlaminck. St. Paul's most prestigious contribution to modern art is the Fondation Maeght, opened in 1964. The buildings merge discreetly into the wooded landscape, and they utilise rainwater to achieve the correct humidity in the galleries. Decorations are by some of the most famous names in present-day art; the courtyard is lined with the filiform statues of Giacometti; the gardens are adorned with fantastic animal figures by Miró whose *La Déese de la Mer* was planted in the sea at Juan-les-Pins in 1968. The Fondation Maeght is committed to all kinds of avant-garde art which seems sometimes to relate less to the immediate environment than to bleaker aspects of the human condition.

No-one can say that the museum-goer is not richly catered for: from local archaeology (Antibes) and local anthropology (anthropoligical museum at Monte-Carlo), to oriental ethnology (Cannes); from art galleries whose pictures are drawn from various schools and

Fondation Maeght, St. Paul; Giacometti figures in the courtyard periods (Monaco and Nice), to exquisitely furnished villas (Musée Ile-de-France at Cap Ferrat), or even imitation Greek (Villa Kerylos, Beaulieu).

But I would like to dwell for a moment on an indigenous art which can be enjoyed at the Musée Masséna in Nice first, and in dozens of churches and chapels in the valleys of the Alpes-Maritimes, as far afield as Genoa. Frescoes and altar-pieces were painted by poor itinerant artists, commissioned by village Brotherhoods of Penitents during the 15th and 16th centuries. A few painted minor masterpieces; most produced an archaic yet original and intensely expressive art of late medieval religious concentration. Their best work was usually on wood; the theme of St. Sebastian recurs, for his arrow-pierced body symbolised the plague—a dreaded visitor. Outstanding among these artists was Louis Bréa, born in Nice in 1443, and dying between 1522 and 1525, his brother Antoine, and Antoine's son François. The group is sometimes called the Bréa School, or the School of Nice Primitives. Louis Bréa's style—tender, softly coloured, soberly realistic, using landscape backgrounds in place of the traditional gold leaf—has led him to be called the Provençal Fra Angelico.

Good examples of the Nice Primitives are in Musée Masséna in Nice; others are in the churches of St. Augustin and St. Barthélemy in Nice, and in the Monastery at Cimiez. The names of a few inland villages can be selected at random; in their churches are fine examples of the School: St. Michael's church at Sospel, the church of St. Véran at Utelle; Lucéram is particularly well endowed; Lieuche, Bonson, Biot, Bouyon, Gréoliéres; one of the most arresting is Notre Dame des Fontaines at La Brigue with quite horrific murals by Baleison and Canavesio, painted between 1480 and 1492—the panel of the suicide of Judas is a fearful vision. So, too, is the *Danse Macabre*, an altarpiece in the Gothic church of Le Bar-sur-Loup; there seemed to be no escape from the plague and damnation.

Going still further back in history are two major Roman remains of the Côte d'Azur. The Roman province of *Alpes maritimae* was administered from Cimiez, *Cemenelum*, whose small arena is less interesting than the baths, the most complete of any Roman baths in France.

La Turbie is far more spectacular. Augustus commemorated his victory over forty-four alpine tribes (their names are known because Pliny the Elder wrote them down) by erecting in 6 B.C. a gigantic monument at the high point of the coast, also the boundary between

Cisalpine Gaul and Transalpine Italy. This *Trophée des Alpes* had been virtually destroyed over the years—blown up, fragments removed for building houses in La Turbie and the original church in Monaco, and parts carted away to Nice and even Genoa—before reconstruction started in 1929. A dramatic approach to the partially restored monument is along Rue Comte-de-Cessole, where a house bears a plaque with a few lines from Dante's *Purgatory* in which he refers to La Turbie. One now has to imagine the monument surmounted by a huge statue of Augustus which stood at the apex of a pyramid of twelve steps. At the foot of the Trophy is the museum which contains a model reconstruction of the original. Travellers today are better served than was Lady Blessington who, avid as always for information, noted on 22nd March, 1823 that the only person who could tell her anything about the monument was a stupid

Partially restored
Roman Trophy of the Alps,
La Turbie

Bronze Age carvings on rocks of Val des Merveilles, Mont Bégo

Saorge suspended above the Roya river

Menton in the 'Bay of Peace' and the autoroute

man at the Custom House who pompously repeated " 'that this was a very fine and ancient ruin, well worth the attention of travellers'. This he reiterated with an air of as much self-complacency as if he had given us the most interesting details".

The last step back in time is the reason for an excursion to the mountains behind Menton. This is not the familiar Provençal landscape, but wild, inhospitable mountain country at between 2,000 and 2,500 metres, an excursion which can be undertaken only in midsummer. Through Sospel and the Gorges de Saorge, and off the main road at St. Dalmas-de-Tende are 300 square kilometres of the Archaeological Zone of Mont Bégo where four valleys contain some 46,000 stereotyped carvings—by no means easy to find—on the naked rock faces. Their repeated geometric forms suggest ideograms, a kind of hieroglyph, but undeciphered. Bovine heads, human figures, spears, hatchets, daggers, axes, forks, ploughs, harrows and simplified cattle enclosure designs are scattered everywhere. The most repeated theme is that of curved horns, lyres, forks or half-moons. Some of the shapes were chipped by Mesolithic man, 7,000 years ago; later ones were worked with iron tools. Who these people were who made these mysterious signs in such stark surroundings is a matter of speculation, but they must have been the predecessors of the Ligurian tribes of the coast who enter the region's earliest history.

First knowledge of the Mont Bégo carvings came at second hand from the 18th century Niçois historian Gioffredo, but in 1952 Jacques Cousteau brought to the surface the log of a ship which around 150 B.C. had been shipwrecked on the rocks of Grand Congloué offshore from Marseille. The log recorded that on the seventy-second day of sailing out of Delos, while offshore from Monaco, Marcus Sestius heard tell of a fearsome summit in the Maritime Alps called Bergos or Beg on which the 'Lygiens practised strange rites and carved signs on the rocks'.

The road back towards Menton winds over the Col de Castillon, past Vieux Castillon, destroyed by the earthquake of 1887, past two curving viaducts that lead nowhere—relics of a tramway which, before 1939, clanked between Menton and Sospel, carrying generations of enthusiastic sightseers slowly past the natural wonders of the region. Set back from the road in the tiny village of Monti is the little hotel called the Pierrot-Pierrette—a few pint-sized bedrooms (and a gill-sized lavatory in the annexe, I distantly remember) and a resourceful and welcoming restaurant.

Then the last five kilometres down to Menton, that little 'outpost of Empire' for older Britons. Under the piers which carry the autoroute from Italy, and along the once enchanting Careï valley. Perhaps, at dusk, Corsica, 160 kilometres away, will surge high out of the mist along the sea's horizon; it is a moment of majestic unbelief. Old Menton lies below, a huddle of honey-warm buildings rising to support the church of St. Michel. Beyond lies the bay, outlined with lights. With unexpected gentleness, the Romans called it *Pacis Sinus*, the Bay of Peace. Where better to end a little tour of Provence?

BIBLIOGRAPHY

It is often said that Provence is a painter's country, but it is also a writer's country, to judge by the richness and diversity of the books to have been written about it. The bibliography below is confined to fairly recent works in English which illuminate the many facets of the region's character.

Among guidebooks, the most useful is in French: *Provence-Côte d'Azur*, Les Guides Bleus: Librairie Hachette, 1971. A somewhat similar, though less informative production in English is *The South of France : Provence and the French Alps*, The Blue Guides: Ernest Benn, 1966. Also available in English is the current edition of *French Riviera*, Michelin Green Guides, whose *Provence* is published only in French.

ALDINGTON, Richard (1956), *Introduction to Mistral*. Heinemann.
DE BEER, Gavin (1967, revised edition), *Hannibal's March*. Sidgwick & Jackson.
DE BEUCKEN, Jean (1962), *Cézanne, a pictorial biography* (translated by Lothian Small). Thames & Hudson.
BOREL, Pierre (1957), *Côte d'Azur* (translated by Alan Ramsay). Nicholas Kaye.
BRANGHAM, A.N. (1962), *The Naturalist's Riviera*. Phoenix House.
BRION, Marcel (1956), *Provence* (translated by S.G. Colverson). Nicholas Kaye.
BRODRICK, A.H. (editor) (1952), *Provence and the Riviera*. Hodder & Stoughton.
CALI, François (1965), *Provence, Land of Enchantment* (translated by E. & A. Heimann). Allen & Unwin.
CAMERON, Roderick (1975), *The Golden Riviera*. Weidenfeld & Nicolson.

Dix, Carol (1975), *The Camargue*. Victor Gollancz.
Droit, Michel (1963), *Camargue* (translated by E. & A. Heimann). Allen & Unwin.
Fearon, Ethelind (1959), *Without my Yacht: how to be at home in the South of France*. Macdonald.
Hanson, Lawrence & Elisabeth (1955), *Portrait of Vincent*. Chatto & Windus with Secker & Warburg.
Higham, Roger (1969), *Provençal Sunshine*. J.M. Dent.
Jackson, Stanley (1975), *Inside Monte Carlo*. W.H. Allen.
Krippner, Monica (1960) *Discovering the Camargue*. Hutchinson.
Lyall, Archibald (1972), *The Companion Guide to the South of France* (revised edition by A.N. Brangham). Collins. (Fontana 1973).
Moyal, Maurice (1956), *On the Road to Pastures New*. Phoenix House.
Parsons, Christopher (1971), *A Bull called Marius*. BBC Publications.
Phillips, Cecilia (1966), *Life in Provence*. Garnstone Press.
Phillips, Cecilia (1975) *Letters from Provence*. Garnstone Press.
Pope-Hennessy, James (1952), *Aspects of Provence*. Longmans.
Pouillon, Fernand (1970), *The Stones of Le Thoronet* (translated by Edward Gillott). Jonathan Cape.
Redfern, W.D. (1967), *The Private World of Jean Giono*. Basil Blackwell.
Rosenbaum, Maurice (1975), *Travellers' Guide to Southern France*. Thornton Cox.
Silvester, Hams (1976) *Horses of the Camargue*. Preface by Konrad Lorenz. Phaidon.
Sussex, R.T. (1966), *Henri Bosco Poet-Novelist*. University of Canterbury, Christchurch, New Zealand.
Turnbull, Patrick (1972), *Provence*. B.T. Batsford.
Weber, Karl & Hoffmann, Lukas (1970), *Camargue* (translated by Ewald Osers). Harrap.
Whelpton, Barbara (1970), *Painter's Provence*. Johnson Publications.
Wylie, Lawrence (1974, third edition), *Village in the Vaucluse*. Harvard University Press.
Yeates, G.K. (1950), *Flamingo City*. Country Life.

INDEX

Aigues-Mortes 32, 97, 98
Aix-en-Provence 27, 33, 34, 35, 36, 102-107, 136
Allemagne-en-Provence 123
Ampus 125
Antibes 148
Apt 28, 30, 70
Arles 28, 29, 32, 35, 44, 85-92
Aubagne 38, 39, 142
Aups 126
Auribeau 71
Avignon 33, 35, 49-52

Barbegal 81
Bargème 125
Bargemon 125
Barjols 38, 117
Barroux 35
Le Bar-sur-Loup 151
La Baume-de-Transit 43
Les Baux 37, 80-81
Beaucaire 13, 32
Beaumes-de-Venise 63
Bédoin 58-59
La Bégude 70
Bollène 44
Bonnieux 26, 69, 72
Boulbon 83
Bourdeaux 13
Brantes 23, 56
Brégançon 134
Briançon 13
Brignoles 29, 37
La Brigue 11, 151

Cabasson 135
Cadenet 67
Cagnes 148, 150
Callas 125
Callian 126
Cannes 36, 133, 149
Cap d'Ail 149
Carcès 114
Caromb 58

Carpentras 33, 35, 59-60
Cassis 132
Castellane 123-124
Castellet 71
Cavaillon 33, 64-65
Céreste 70
Chamaret 43
Champtercier 121
Chantemerle-lès-Grignan 43
Chastellard-de-Lardiers 26
Château-Arnoux 110
Châteauneuf-du-Pape 49
Châteauvert 114
Cimiez 148, 151
Comps-sur-Artuby 125
Correns 114
Cotignac 117
Crestet 63
Cruis 110

Défilé de Mirabeau 113
Dieulefit 13, 40, 42, 53
Digne 15, 33, 120
Draguignan 114, 117

Entremont 27
Esparron 114
l'Estagnol 134
Eze 33

Fayence 126
Figanières 125
Flayosc 117
Fontaine-de-Vaucluse 38, 42
Fontvieille 81
Forcalquier 72, 110, 111-112, 118
Fos-sur-Mer 39
Fréjus 116, 118-119, 149
Fréjus-Plage 28, 39

Gap 13
Gardanne 38
La Garde-Adhémar 43, 44

La Garde-Freinet 30
Gargas 71
Gigondas 62
Gilette 33
Gordes 26, 35, 72
Golfe-Juan 37
Gourdon 33
Grand Congloué 156
Grasse 15, 38
Gréoux-les-Bains 123
Grignan 42
Grottes de Calès 25

Hyères 36, 128, 133

Jougues 113

Lacoste 65
Lafare 63
Lamanon 25
Lauris 66
Le Lavandou 132
Lavéra 39
Lorgues 115
Lourmarin 35, 69

Maillane 83
Malaucène 55, 63
Mane 110
Manosque 64, 112-113
Marseille 11, 27, 29, 35, 38, 136-140
Mazan 56
Ménerbes 65
Menton 11, 31, 36, 129, 146, 149, 156
Mérindol 35
Meyrargues 113
Mons 119
Mont Bégo 26, 155-156
Montauroux 126
Montélimar 42
Montfort-sur-Argens 114
Monti 156

159

Montmajour 83
Mormoiron 58
Moustiers-Ste. Marie 123, 124

Nice 35, 36, 127, 133, 145-146, 151
Nîmes 28, 77
Notre Dame des Lumieres 71, 110
Nyons 42, 53

Orange 27, 28, 42, 45-49

Le Pègue 53
Pennafort 122
Pernes-les-Fontaines 31, 35, 59
Pont du Gard 11
Pont Julien 28, 70
Pont St. Esprit 11
Port Cros 133
Port Grimaud 132

Richerenches 43
Riez 122
La Roque-Alric 63
La Roque-d'Anthéron 66
Roquebrune-Cap Martin 24
Roquebrune-sur-Argens 116
Roussillon 71
Rustrel 71

Sablet 63
Saignon 71
Salernes 117
Sault-de-Vaucluse 56
Séguret 63
Seillons-Source-d'Argens 117
Serignan-du-Comtat 44, 45
Sigale 33
Sillans-la-Cascade 117
Signal de Lure 110
Sisteron 56, 108-109
Solérieux 43
Sorgues 49
Suze-la-Rousse 43, 44
Suzette 63
Sylveréal 97

St. Antonin-du-Var 115
St. Auban 110
St. Blaise 27
Ste. Cécile-les-Vignes 44
St. Christol 56
St. Etienne-des-Orgues 110
St. Gilles 32
St. Jean-de-Garguier 142
St. Léger-du-Ventoux 56
Les. Stes. Maries-de-la-Mer 30, 95-97, 99, 132
St. Martin-de-Pallières 114
St. Maximin 117

St. Michel-l' Observatoire 17, 110
St. Paul-Trois-Châteaux 43, 44
St. Raphaël 116
St. Rémy-de-Provence 73
St. Restitut 44
St. Tropez 35, 128, 147

Tarascon 13, 34, 81, 82, 83
Taulignan 42
Tende 11
Toulon 35, 37
Tourrettes 126
Tourtour 125
La Traconnade 113
La Turbie 151-152

Vaison-la-Romaine 28, 54
Valensole 121-122
Valaurie 43
Vallauris 148
Valréas 43
Varages 114
Venasque 30, 59
Vence 149
Vidauban 115
Villefranche 149
Villeneuve-lès-Avignon 52
Villes-sur-Auzon 56
Volonne 109

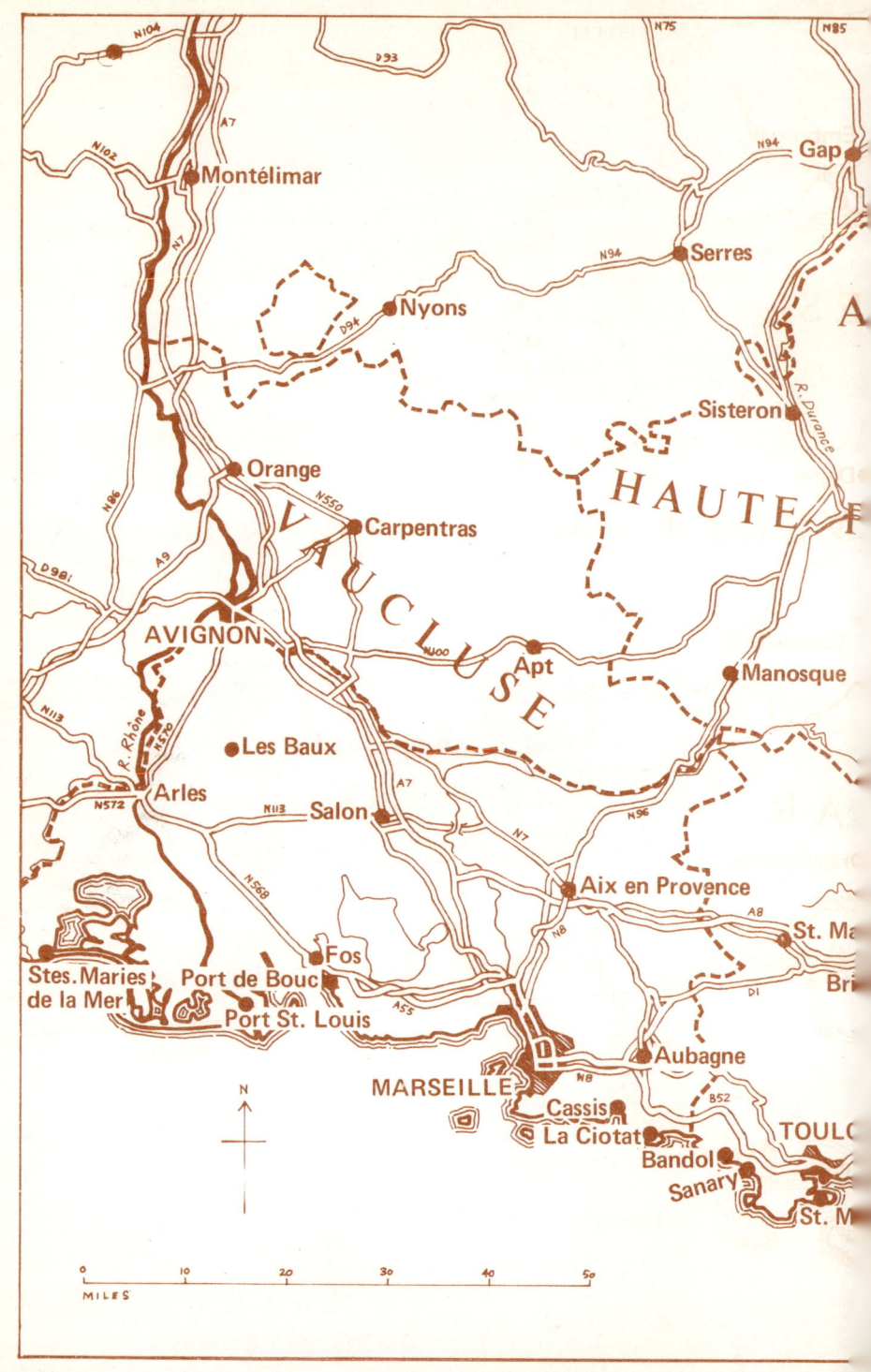